Stand TALL and STRAIGHT

Stand TALL and STRAIGHT

A design for the man you want to become

by Bill Glass

with Dr. Leslie E. Moser and Stan Moser

Library of Congress Catalog Card Number: 67-23974

First Printing, May 1967
Second Printing, October 1967
Third Printing, April 1968

Contents

PART TWO:
YOU CAN DEVELOP A DYNAMIC PERSONALITY

PART THREE:
HOW TO BUILD A HEALTHY AND POWERFUL BODY

PART FOUR:
YOU AND THE PEOPLE AROUND YOU

PART FIVE:
YOU AND YOUR VALUES

A WORD FROM BILL GLASS

We all have our problems. The problems I have as defensive end for the Cleveland Browns facing people like Jim Taylor and Jim Parker across the line of scrimmage are plenty tough. Believe me when one of those guys comes at you, you've got problems. They are just as big and just as tough as I am, and they are just as determined to do their jobs. If it's Jim Taylor's job to make that first down, it's my job to stop him. If it's Don Meredith's job to throw that touchdown pass to Hayes, it's my job to stop him. And don't forget that a two hundred-sixty pound tackle is determined to keep me from hitting Meredith. I only have four seconds to beat him and get there.

But you have your problems, too; and I don't envy you either. You are going to have plenty of tough opponents facing you as you get down on the field of life and try to be a winner. I would like to be able to help you in your struggle to become a man — and maybe I can.

Here's how it all started

A few months ago I met Dr. Leslie Moser in the Baylor Drug Store just off the Baylor University campus. My family and I had just returned to Waco for the off season, which we have been doing for several years.

I played college football at Baylor before entering pro football and Dr. Moser, a prominent psychologist, was a professor there. Unfortunately, we didn't get together until last year.

When I met Dr. Moser, he had just finished his fourth book, each of which is devoted to counseling with young people. Then for some reason I said, "Say, Doctor, why don't we write a book together?" That's the way it started.

Before I left Waco to go back to training camp, we had decided on the book we wanted to write. Both of us were interested in the same thing—we wanted to write to help young men like you become the finest men possible. We decided to call the book *STAND*

TALL AND STRAIGHT, A Design for the Man You Want To Become, because we believe that every one of you really desires to grow into a man who can look the world in the eye and stand tall and straight before God and your fellow men.

The book you have in your hand would not have been possible without the careful planning and outlining Dr. Moser did. Being a psychologist and an accomplished writer, he has been able to organize the contents of this book in a way that only a scholar could.

Stan Moser enters the picture

But you will notice that this book has three authors. As the book began to take shape we spent a lot of time at Dr. Moser's house; and since his son, Stan, was seventeen, we realized that he was part of the audience for the book. Stan was reading what we had written, and had some good ideas. We thought we could use those ideas in the book.

So the third author, Stan Moser, entered the picture. Stan was a senior in Richfield High School at Waco, Texas, at the time. It was exciting to work with Stan and get his views on things. It hasn't been long since I was a teen-ager, and I spend a lot of time with teen-agers now. But to have one of you guys actually help in the writing is the best idea I could possibly imagine. Stan enthusiastically accepted the challenge to help us.

So, guys, there are three authors of this book, each serving a slightly different purpose. I will be speaking to you straight from the shoulder. But everything I say to you will be based on the sound foundation of Dr. Moser's knowledge and experience in psychology. And Stan will be looking over both our shoulders putting in his interpretations and impressions.

I want you to know that we are trying hard to make these tough teen-age years happier and better for you. This book is designed especially for you, the young men in whose hands the future of mankind lies.

Here's What We Are Going To Talk About in This Book

Christ wants all of us to live abundantly

Have you ever felt you were missing something in life? Have you felt you weren't really alive? The first thing we are going to do is try to make you aware of what a great privilege it is to be alive. Some say that this is a terrible time in which to live. We don't believe it! We believe Christ has come to make living in this world *now* a thrilling challenge. We are enjoying our lives and we want you to enjoy yours. So, in the first part of the book we are going to show you how to live abundantly by following Jesus Christ.

You can develop a dynamic personality

Have you wanted the kind of personality that will really make you a winner? Have you wanted to improve your personality, but just haven't known how to do it? We are going to tell you how you can do this and much more in Part Two of this book. We will be drawing on all of the knowledge of religion, psychology, and good old common sense in order to show you how you can learn to *be a winner by developing a dynamic personality.*

You can develop a powerful and beautiful body

Have you wished that you had a body of which you could be truly proud? We know that you can't be really alive unless you have a powerful and healthy body. So we are giving you seven big chapters in Part Three dealing with every phase of body building. We'll tell you about conditioning, isometrics, and weight lifting. We'll talk with you about eating right and about good health habits.

You need a strong body to live successfully and to be of maximum service; and you can have it, if you will just follow the instructions faithfully. You'll really be anxious to read Part Three!

You must get along with people

Have you wanted better grades, a good job, and more loyal friends? Have you wanted to really get along with your parents? The world you live in is full of people—people of all types. You've got to learn how to get along with people to make it in this world of great joys and hard knocks.

We will tell you how to deal with all kinds of people—your parents, teachers, adult men and women, and your friends. Each type person requires a slightly different approach, and we want you to be prepared to cope with any person you meet. Read Part Four carefully—you might want to read it twice.

You must learn about values

Have you wanted to know the truth about drinking and smoking? Or have you ever wondered whether a certain thing was right or wrong? The thing that stands in the way of so many guys is confusion concerning what is right and wrong, good and bad, desirable and undesirable. You live in a world of values; and often you just don't know which way to turn. Christ gave us instruction in the Bible about the values we should embrace; but then, there are many things we just have to figure out for ourselves.

What kind of girls should you keep company with? What do you owe your parents? What kind of social life should you lead? These are questions that require you to make value judgments.

In Part Five of this book, we are going to help you interpret Christ's teachings as they apply to you today. Don't miss Part Five!

You must understand your sexual nature

Have you ever wanted a girl to like you? Have you ever wanted to know how to get a date? The final sections in this book will deal with your relationships with the opposite sex. This is a really important part of your lives. We'll tell you what we think about the so-called "sex revolution" in America. We'll give you the facts about sex as straight from the shoulder as we know how. You'll find all of this and more in Parts Six and Seven.

We believe you'll get something from every page. We are really anxious for you to read this book and understand what we are talking about when we urge you to *stand tall and straight*. We want you to understand fully our idea of *a design for a man*—the man we want you to become.

PART ONE

You and Your World—God's Creation

1

Living Abundantly Means Living Enthusiastically

Did you ever trade licks with a friend? You get the first lick, and man, do you unload on him! He waits a long time before he hits you and you are saying, "Come on, come on, and get it over with." You are really dreading his blow.

You may get hit fifty times during a football game harder than he'll hit you. But you are so excited about winning that game that you don't dread the body punishment at all. You usually don't even think about getting hurt. In fact, you get to where you enjoy the contact.

What's the difference in these two situations? In one word—enthusiasm!!

I am convinced that Jesus Christ lived enthusiastically. Right now, I want you to adopt for your own life the idea of enthusiastic, abundant life. We don't have an actual photograph of Jesus, but all the word pictures we do have show Him to be a man of power, physical strength, and virility. He wasn't a quiet docile person with a "give-up" approach to life. He was a winner.

Most of the time Christ was gentle. He loved people, but He hated hypocrisy. Once, He grabbed a whip and drove the money changers out of the temple. He could rise to any occasion, and there is every reason to believe that He really enjoyed being alive. And remember, He said, "I have come that ye might have life and have it more abundantly."

Now, again, this is the theme of the book we are writing—to show you how to live with zip and zest, how to take the teachings of Christ and apply them to your own lives. You may be sure that in every sense of the word He stood "tall and straight."

If you are going to help people, the worst possible thing is for you to live like a whipped dog with your tail between your legs. Christ doesn't want us to be sorrowful and sad. He wants us to be exuberant—to show the world that being a Christian is to be *really alive*. I know God can depend on each of you to show the world that Christ's way is the exciting way.

Every one of you guys has a different way of reacting to the world around you. Some of you are naturally cautious and insecure, lacking confidence in anything or anybody. Many of you are elated, optimistic, and enthusiastic about everything you try. Nothing will block your way to success.

What makes you the way you are? You are what you are to some extent because of the way your glands secrete hormones into your bloodstream. Also allow some influence from the body you have been walking around in for the last ten years.

Your outlook has also been developed by your early experiences as a child and by the things you have picked up from the people you have been around for any length of time. You are all the people you ever met, including God, rolled into one. Or, as I heard someone say, "You *are* what you've been becoming–the decisions you, alone, have made; the things you've thought about; the people you've chosen for your pattern."

Well, here you are just becoming a man and you've already built something of a plan for your life. You probably aren't a total optimist or a total pessimist. You are somewhere between the extremes of a cautious, insecure pessimist, who expects the worst and usually finds it, and the enthusiastic optimist, who sees the world as a warm friendly place full of great people. The question you must ask yourself is, "Will the pattern of life I have developed make me happy or will I just exist in boredom or unhappiness?"

In baseball there was a time when people said, "The Yankees get all the breaks." Now, they are saying the same thing about Green Bay in football. But I really believe that a team makes its own breaks. The optimistic and enthusiastic person gets the breaks because he makes them, just as a good football team does.

Enthusiasm and optimism are important

If you are a young man who feels as if he is carrying the burdens of the whole world on his shoulders, why don't you make some changes? Changes aren't difficult at your age; but they will be almost impossible twenty years from now. And just think of all the fun you'll miss if you don't change.

It's hard to know what is really important, but a pretty good way to measure success in living is to check the level of happiness and the feeling of satisfaction you have each day you live. When you become an elderly person, if you have to look back on a life that was filled with unhappiness and depression, you would rightly call your life a failure. If you look back on days filled with enjoyment, enthusiasm, and accomplishment, you could rightly say, "I really did all right, didn't I?" I'm sure you'd rather be an optimist—there's no reason for you to waste your life looking at the bad in everything.

You can do something about it

If you were on your way to play in a big game and you got off on the wrong exit, you'd just go back to the intersection and get on the right street. That's just what you're going to have to do if you're going to discover a way to live an enthusiastic life.

Suppose your team really takes a licking. In the dressing room the best thing to do is to keep your mouth shut. Many times you say things you shouldn't say, and do things you shouldn't do because you're so disgusted. But as time goes on, the hurt wears off. Then you ask yourself, "Why did we lose?" You learn from your mistakes; then you decide to win the next time. It gets to burning

deep down in your guts, and you feel you must win next time. And usually you do win, if you feel like that.

But some few of you are rebelling against your society. You are wearing your hair long, and you're carrying placards and rebelling. When you rebel against society, you rebel primarily against yourself, because when you are against people you are hurting yourself more than anyone.

If you have been seeing the world around you as a real bore and you react negatively, you have simply developed a bad habit. You must break this habit just as you would stop biting your nails. It won't be easy, but you can do it.

Why not start each day off with a little pep talk to yourself. Decide within yourself that you're going to have a good day. The world around you is filled with both pleasant and unpleasant things; but you have a right to make your private world the way *you* want it. The only catch is that it becomes your responsibility to make it the way *you* want it. The person who fails to take advantage of this privilege is much like the old lady who walks up to a senator in time of a crisis and says, "It's not my fault, the shape this country's in, because I'm seventy-eight years old, and I haven't voted even once."

In other words, your life can be cold and gloomy, or it can be warm and inviting, according to your effort. The pep talk you give yourself should evolve quickly into imagination. Just imagine what's going to happen during the day and see yourself in imagination doing a good job and having a great time. If you should picture an unhappy moment, replace it with a picture of success. Close this preparation time with prayer and take off!

Many times throughout the pages of this book, I will be suggesting to you that you will live a fuller life if you start your day off right. You are going to be facing many difficult times when you are going to be under pressure. These situations will be much easier for you, if you will get into the habit of starting your day off right. This means getting into the proper frame of mind; and the time to get yourself straight for the day's activity is bright and early in the morning.

Maybe you've got a big test, a big game, or an oral report to make. It is important that you get your feet under you, get your self-confidence running strong, and above all, *get on God's side!*

After you read your Bible (I suggest a modern version), why not make it a habit to read also the testimony of at least one great Christian athlete each morning. You will find these testimonies in two books published in conjunction with the Fellowship of Christian Athletes. They are titled THE GOAL AND THE GLORY and COURAGE TO CONQUER. I would also like to recommend THE BOBBY RICHARDSON STORY and HEART OF A CHAMPION. The last one was written by Bob Richards, an Olympic champion.

The testimonies in these books are very brief, and they let you know what a lot of fine Christian athletes think about life. This type of reading will help you know how the great athletes of our country take their Christian faith with them into the locker room and onto the playing field. You can find these books at almost any bookstore.

You might want to become a member of the Fellowship of Christian Athletes. For a very small fee (two dollars per year) you will receive the magazine called THE CHRISTIAN ATHLETE. It carries a daily devotional. Order it from *The Christian Athlete,* Suite 812, Traders National Bank Building, 1125 Grand Avenue, Kansas City, Missouri, 64106.

You might, also, want to read my own book, GET IN THE GAME! I am working on another book which I am tentatively calling INSIDE PRO FOOTBALL. Get these at your bookstore, also.

You must be realistic even though optimistic

Of course you know that you can't ignore your problems because you are always going to have your share of trouble. You can't and shouldn't hide your head from reality like an ostrich hides his head in the sand.

Sure, you're going to face some hard knocks; you can't escape all the bruises, but your basic attitudes can be positive. Even when you do become happy with yourself, you still can't ignore the cold realities of a mixed-up world. You simply have to deal with these problems as you must and refuse to let your confidence in the basic goodness of life be shaken. You lose some battles; but you'll never lose the war.

There are many reasons you should be optimistic and enthusiastic

The "beatniks" of our generation seem to feel that there is no use in struggling. "The world is in a mess," they say, so they beat their bongos, grow their beards, and blame someone else for their troubles. They can't seem to find anything other than griping and rebelling which makes them happy. You must become part of the solution to world problems, and avoid being part of the problem itself.

God still is in charge

The ultimate decision in our world is not going to be made in Moscow by the Premier, nor will it be made in Washington by the President. The ultimate decision in our world is going to be made by God. He has always been the ultimate power, and He always will be. Certainly everything in our world is not "all right," but God has not given up His world and He will always be in control, no matter what. If I didn't believe that, I'd be shaking in my boots. But since I do, my main concern is to be involved in becoming part of the solution to the world's problems. Your faith in God makes it possible for you to work for a good life and expect to have it.

It's difficult to understand the beatniks and others like them because there is so much for which we have to be thankful. The poet has written, "My heart leaps up when I behold a rainbow in the sky." If you have the right attitude, your heart will leap up daily —you will look for and find all the wonderful things around you.

2

Let The World Know You Are Happy

I don't care how long I play pro football, when I'm introduced and run down between the goal posts to join my teammates for the game, I get goose pimples. My heart begins to keep time with the excitement of the crowd, and I literally tremble with the enthusiasm of the game. This state continues until late that night, after the game has been history for hours.

You can't get to this fever pitch every day, but with a little practice the enthusiastic approach will come easy to you. And when this becomes your pattern for living, you will find that people will be glad to have you around. They will respond to you, they will admire and respect you. Most important of all, they'll like you. Furthermore, they will follow your example toward a similar life.

People must see your enthusiasm

I was recently watching a bunch of high school football players come into the dressing room to get ready for practice. The first guy came stumbling through the door with a loud sigh, flopped down onto the bench in front of his locker, and began lazily to put on his equipment. The next guy came in dragging his feet with his head hung low, threw his books down on the bench, and sat down beside the first. A little later, two other players came stumbling in. They both walked slowly and aimlessly into the room.

And then, a guy bounded into the room and jumped over a couple of benches. With a good word for one of his teammates, a handshake for another one, with a smile for everybody—you guessed it, he pepped up the whole atmosphere. I went over and shook hands with this guy and said, "Buddy I want to meet you." I hate to say it, but as for the rest of those deadbeats, I couldn't have cared less.

You can't keep from showing the world how you really feel. It's reflected in the excitement of your smile, the spring in your step. Naturally, you wouldn't want to be phony by showing a back-slapping, jovial front all the time. But, on the other hand your natural enthusiasm for life will definitely show.

There is nothing that will help you more than a cheerful disposition. Let your enthusiasm come through to people around you. An enthusiastic optimist moves with head held high and shoulders back. He's a winner and he knows it.

A cheerful disposition will conquer many problems that might otherwise get you down.

Sometimes it helps to detour

There are several ways to meet the problems which you meet daily. The best approach to any problem is direct attack (seeing what needs to be done and doing it). Sometimes, however, it is necessary to use the detour method to by-pass an obstacle. This is all right as long as you detour only to find a better way to overcome your problem. If you wanted to go outside you wouldn't run through the wall, you'd go through the door. The closest way is through the wall, but the best way is through the door.

Let's suppose you've made a bad grade in English. You feel like really telling that teacher what you think. You don't think she graded your theme fairly. What do you do?

Well, I'd say that you ought to take a detour. Instead of charging up to her and complaining, take a detour. Why not arrange to run into her in the hall, at the water fountain, maybe? Greet her courteously, be sure to smile, and start your detour. You know where you are going—you are trying to understand her point of view, and at the same time get her to see things your way. Eventually, you wind up at her desk telling her in a nice way that you think she was too tough when she graded your paper. But that detour keeps the teacher on your side as you move toward mutual understanding.

There are good and bad ways to handle any problem

Anybody can retreat from his problems, but the method of giving up is usually a bad approach to any situation. Rationalizing, or making up excuses for your failure to overcome difficulties is also a bad approach, although it might be all right if you didn't carry it too far. If you want to see this done to the degree where it becomes science, you should see players making excuses on film day for not getting a block or making a tackle. Some are genuine reasons, but many are just excuses. Sure, I'm as guilty as anybody else! I once heard a coach describe a player like this, "He makes very few mistakes, in fact, he makes almost no mistakes. At least, we can't get him to admit any." If you rationalize, it should sound something like this, "Why did I fail to make that tackle? Because I closed my eyes? From now on I'm going to stare at that ball carrier's belt buckle and I won't miss." This is constructive rationalization. But if you are unwilling to admit your mistake you can never improve.

Daydreaming as a solution to a problem is not good either, unless you dream about how you are going to do it better the next time, and then fly into action and tackle the problem.

Don't be afraid of your problems. Go out and try to beat them; don't let them beat you. Be smart about it—take the easiest way so long as it really works; but always conquer those difficulties one way or another.

Remember, Christ wasn't a quitter—neither should you be. He was a winner. He won the greatest victory of all, a victory over death. And He extends His spirit and example of victorious living to you and to me.

During the football season I was asked to go and visit a little boy in the hospital who had a terminal case of cancer. I bounced into the room and stuck out my hand to shake his; and then I realized that the cancer had progressed so far that he didn't even have the strength to raise his arm up to shake my hand. But he was living a day at a time—he was enjoying my visit because he loved the Cleveland Browns and wanted to talk football. We talked for quite some time about the Browns' opportunity to win the championship that year. He was very enthusiastic and tried to encourage me to do my best in the game that was coming up.

I went in to try and encourage *him,* but I went out very highly encouraged, because I really began to be a little bit grateful for what God had given me—a strong, healthy body, a free country, a healthy family, and the opportunity to play a wonderful game like football.

You and I take a lot of things for granted. We don't really appreciate them until we see someone who doesn't have the things we have. You don't appreciate your wonderful school unless you read of, or meet, people who are deprived of such a school. You don't really appreciate your health, your parents, your country, or the freedom to worship as you please until you lose these freedoms or until they are threatened.

You don't really learn to appreciate freedom of speech until you lose it. In fact, some people abuse freedom of speech. They think that freedom means license; and, therefore, they yell curse words in public, thinking this means freedom of speech.

Sure, we have our problems, and I know that you might want to rebel at times, but we still are the greatest country in the world with the greatest opportunities and the greatest freedoms. We ought to appreciate what we have and try to use it in the best possible way.

I say it again because I think it is important: We ought to be part of the solution to the world's problems rather than part of the problem itself. You probably are in the upper five per cent of the world in educational opportunities and standard of living. I wonder how you are going to use all these advantages.

Nature is full of wonders, and the world is full of wonderful people who, though far from being perfect, are still loved by God. In our land of freedom we have plenty of material things to enjoy, we have freedom of speech and of worship. In spite of a few rotten eggs the world is good, and God is sufficient to keep it that way. Always consider pain, heartache, and disappointment to be only temporary affairs and live with the expectation that the sun will break through whatever clouds may come into your life. Live with enthusiasm; it's contagious.

3

You Are Something Very Special

To tell the truth, I've missed a lot of routine tackles. Or you might say I've fumbled the ball plenty of times. "Well," you say, "Everybody does—it's natural. You can learn more from these mistakes than any other way."

You're right! Learning from your mistakes is fine. But I still wish I had had someone to help me a little more with my problems when I was growing up. So, for that reason, I want to sit down and talk to you personally about some of the things I think will make the game you play at home, at school, on the field, and everywhere a lot more victorious for you.

God is running this show, and it is up to you to figure out where you fit into it all. The biggest question in your life is what kind of man you are going to make. Your quest for learning everything about yourself is never-ending, but can be truly rewarding.

The time comes in every boy's life when he must realize and accept the fact that soon he will become a man. Take a long close look at yourself. Right now, you have the body and the mind that will also belong to you when you are a fully grown man. No other person has the same qualities as you; and no other person will develop his qualities quite like you. One of your biggest jobs in life is to find yourself. You must find out who you really are, and decide which way you want to go.

Only human beings can think about such things

Perhaps this seems to be a very unusual thing for you to be thinking about. After all, you may have really never stopped to think about who you are or why you are here. The future holds many new and interesting things; but up to now you have been content to accept things on a daily come-what-may basis, and you have never made any plans about your development as a person or a Christian.

You have the ability as a human being to stand aside and look yourself over. No other creature besides the human being can do this, so really take a close look.

Descartes, a famous French philosopher, once stated, "I am because I think." Sure this sounds like a history lesson, but this bit of history *can* be applied. You see, there may not be too much we can really know about this life, but we do know we exist. This wise old man started with this premise and proceeded to prove that there is a God.

It may surprise you, but you really know very little about yourself. You know that you are alive, and that you can control yourself in most ways. But another thing that's very important is the direction in which you lead yourself.

This life is yours; this body is yours; this mind is yours; and the control of all of these things is yours only because God gave these things to you along with the power to control them. It is strictly up to you to study and learn the plan God has for your life. Then you must carry out this plan, because you have the opportunity during the next few years to build the man who can look back on a life of happiness and productivity knowing that you have met the obstacles and have grown into what you were created to be. And if you are fulfilling the purpose for your creation in the first place, then, buddy, you're really living. You are a real man.

Now is the time to start to develop into a mature Christian

This real success of a creature becoming what you were created to be must include faith in a Supreme Being. Everything around you at this present time indicates that someone or something must have a hand in it all. You and your environment exist in such an amazing orderliness that you are bound to know there is a Supreme Being behind it all. As the Bible says, "The fool hath said in his heart, there is no God."

Suppose you and I were standing on my front porch, and there was a car parked at the curb. It wasn't like any car you had ever seen, so you asked, "Bill, what kind of car is that?"

"Oh," I'd say, "that's no kind of car."

You'd say, "It's got to be some kind of car, Bill. Its got to be a Ford, a Chevrolet, a Dodge, or something."

"No," I'd say, "that's my accidental car."

"What in the world are you talking about?" You'd say. "I never heard of such a thing." In fact you'd begin to think this hot Texas sun had shot my brain, but good.

I'd say, "If you like, I'll tell you what happened. Well, one day I was standing here in my front yard and a big four-barrel 428 engine came sliding down the hill. Up popped a chassis under this motor, and four mag wheels came rolling out of the woods and hooked on. Then the body came whirling over the top of the house, fenders came out of nowhere, the Texas wind whipped nuts and bolts around like a whirlwind; it's amazing what these West Texas winds can blow up, and 'presto'—there was my 'accidental' car."

I can just hear you gasping, "Man! What a liar! That's the biggest lie I ever heard even a Texan tell."

My car was made by General Motors Corporation and to say it's accidental is ridiculous, but it seems to me that it is a billion times more ridiculous to say that our universe is an accident.

Just as certainly as design demands a designer, creation demands a Creator. The universe has such fantastic precision that you could set your watch to the minute by where a distant star would be a hundred years from now. All of this universe is no accident.

If the facts about the immediate world around you were not enough to convince you of the presence of a Supreme Being, the hours you have spent in church studying your faith may have influenced you some. Your parents have probably related to you the story of Jesus, and the manner in which he lived, died, and rose again that we may be forgiven of our sins.

You have probably heard of Jesus all your life, and you have committed your life to Him. In the coming years, you will more and more rely on the things you have learned and the faith you have developed to help you overcome life's many hazards and probelms.

Manhood—the supreme accomplishment

It is quite frightening to know that you have the capability and the responsibility to perform a special purpose in life. But suppose you had never existed. That would really have been a tragedy! The challenge of exploration is before you. You must follow and fulfill this challenge, or it would have been better if you had never even existed.

During your search for the answers to your true purpose for life, you must learn more and more things about yourself as a person. Right now you know very little. You know that you have parents and that they are reasonably good parents; but you know little about yourself. You can't see the future, so you can only watch yourself develop now. This development must be strictly natural, as God intended it; but you must be the architect, chief engineer, and builder, who molds the natural resources into the finished product. Unless you put forth a supreme effort to mold a man out of your possibilities, the final product will not be satisfying to you.

Actually, you should think of yourself as a very lucky and special person. You are like a person beginning a big-game hunt. You don't know exactly what lies ahead, but you do know that it involves adventure, and you are prepared to cope with what may come—to use your natural abilities to make the best of the expedition. When it is all over, you will be able to look in the mirror and know that you are the best man you could be. You will have used your talents and reached your goals in life.

What determines your greatness?

But hold it a minute! Before you even begin your expedition into manhood, you must remember the most important thing of all: greatness is not measured in money, land, or other material wealth. God looks on the inward heart. He doesn't care if you wear a new silk suit or a towsack. You become great in God's sight when you have done your best to find His plan for your life and live up to it with His strength.

How will you ever know if you're finding His plan and living by it? One way to determine if you have really achieved your greatness will be by the feeling inside you. If you are happy and contented that is a good sign. You can be happy with the lowest position in the world if you are finding your place in life as God intended it. Another check would be to square your life with what He has shown to you in the Bible. Remember, Christ said, "Whosoever would be greatest in the Kingdom of God, let him become a servant." In other words greatness lies in service to God, mankind, and yourself.

You will find greatness if you become the unique person you are destined to be and if you are valuable both to yourself and to mankind. In doing so, you will also be serving God. If you are usually happy and feel worthwhile, you are hitting pretty close to the mark.

Now, don't miss it! Happiness comes as a by-product of a fruitful life. If your happiness is genuine, you can be sure it is coming from a fruitful life. But if you are happy *only* when you are involved in a fun thing or when you are satisfying some hunger or drive, then something is wrong. A great man said: "You don't find happiness looking for it; you stumble over it on the road to duty." The textbooks say it a little differently, but it means the same thing: "The happy person is the one intent on achieving his goals."

4

You Must Learn to Appreciate Yourself

The Bible says that you as a Christian should love your neighbor "as you love yourself." You may have thought that this means you should think very little of yourself in order to love your neighbor more. But it more likely means that you should love and appreciate yourself more so that you can, in turn, love and appreciate your neighbor more.

How could you possibly love others if you don't love yourself? A person who doesn't love himself can actually become dangerous to himself and to others. If you don't appreciate yourself, then you won't care for anyone else either, and no one will like you. That's just plain logic.

I know you are smart enough to realize, however, that you could be so self-centered that you wouldn't have time or energy to think about anyone else. Self-love carried too far is usually referred to in the Bible as "pride." We might call it "foolish pride," which would indicate the wrong kind of self-appreciation. You've got to love yourself if you're going to have a real sense of worth; but not so much that you become self-centered.

What we are trying to do in this book is to show you how you can have a really enjoyable life and be the very best man you can. But first you must realize that living happily and having all you want is impossible unless you are in harmony with those who are your most constant companions.

You must think positively about yourself

Think! Who is your most constant companion? You are, of course. You must live with yourself twenty-four hours a day, so you must get to like the guy in your skin.

Look yourself over and be prepared to make the best of what you are and of what you may become. True, you are what you are. But you can become more what you ought to be. What you are can be great if you'll just learn to build up the positive and eliminate the negative.

Maybe you aren't everything you could hope to be. There isn't a single one of us who doesn't want some qualities that we don't have and never could have. Maybe you wish for a stronger, more muscular physique, maybe you wish you were more intelligent, and certainly you wish that you were more handsome. Well, I'm sure you can be more what you really want to be, but there really may not be anything wrong with you the way you are. So often you hear people say, "Just don't worry—be yourself." Well, that's a pretty good philosophy up to a point.

But I've noticed that so many of you guys use this as an excuse—"That's just the way I am," turns out to mean, "that's the way I'm going to keep on being." You see, this can be an excuse not to put out the effort to overcome mediocrity. If you say, "that's just the way I am" as an excuse, you're as good as dead in that particular area of life.

Too often, you settle for second best. You're confusing the idea of being your mediocre self with the idea of being your *best* self. I'm convinced that Jimmy Brown is the greatest athlete that ever lived. But in my opinion, even he used a very small percentage of his capabilities; yet, he probably used a greater percentage of his ability than any athlete who ever lived.

I feel that God expects us to be our very best selves and to use our talents to His glory in whatever we may seek to do. Be realistic but be honest. Don't settle for second best in those areas of life where you can really become great!

You must endeavor to change some things and to be content with others

There are at least two things to keep firmly in mind as you try to live with yourself and learn to really enjoy it. There are some things you can do to move toward your ideal. But on the other hand, there are other things with which you will just have to be content.

Let's take the physical. The body you have is a combination of heredity and early environment. You have body proportions handed down from your parents. These things embedded in your cells determine what you can be but not necessarily what you will be. You may have inherited the capacity for being six feet tall. This means you couldn't under the very best conditions be six feet one inch, and that you will in probability not even reach the full possibility of six feet.

But it is certainly not all heredity. You can develop yourself tremendously as a physical specimen by the right diet and exercise, always pressing toward the limitations caused by your heredity. So, you really should develop the very best body you can. Don't be content until you've done everything possible to develop your body. In Part Three I'll tell you how you can become a physical powerhouse.

Many of you guys who have somewhat scrawny bodies are tremendously unhappy and feel that life has passed you by. You look jealously at the tremendous bodies of your friends and feel beat. But stop and think! This body of yours, which may not look like much, may have the qualities that will give you perfect health for nearly a hundred years. The beautiful body of your friend may have internal weaknesses that don't show, but that will be responsible for his having a heart attack when he is thirty-five. You just can't tell by looking. But if you really want to, and, if you aren't sick, you can develop your body beyond belief.

Dick Shaffrath came to play with the Browns back in 1959. The first day he walked into training camp and said he wanted to play offensive tackle at 210 pounds people almost laughed. But he displayed so much bull-dog determination that he made the club. This in itself was quite impressive considering the fact that most pro tackles weigh above 245 and up to 285.

After that first year the coaches sent him home saying, "Son, go home and grow up." And he did! He went home and lifted weights. And boy did he lift weights! He got to where he was bench pressing over 400 pounds. He worked on the weights, and paid special attention to his diet. He ate between four and six meals a day. He gulped protein and every kind of food supplement imaginable.

When he walked into training camp seven months later, it created a real uproar. He weighed 260 pounds, was hard as a rock, and faster than ever. He is now an All Pro offensive tackle.

In the mental realm it is much the same thing. Here, however, the hereditary factor may be little more of a problem. You do inherit your basic mental abilities to a large degree; and these powers aren't quite as subject to improvement through your own efforts as may be the case with the physical body. On the other hand, no person ever uses all his brain power, and you can certainly train yourself to use a larger portion of yours. They say Einstein, the famous physicist and mathematician, used only about ten percent of his mental capacity. Well, you may need to use ninety percent of yours to do your job, but don't quit until you use everything you've got.

You must be realistic about your aspirations

Still at the same time, you must not be too hard on yourself. You can't keep your nose in a book constantly, and you may just have to be content with average grades while some sharper people around you get the A's. Don't let this get you down. Be realistic. Work as hard as you can; and then accept yourself as you are and as you dream of becoming, making a constant effort both mentally and physically.

You experience the world through your body

The Bible says that the body is "the temple of the soul." Realizing this, you can't cheat your body and expect a satisfying life. You must appreciate this body God has given, you must improve it in every possible way; and you must be proud of it.

The real you is not physical, it is mental and spiritual. But you must experience life to a large degree with your body. You can't split yourself up; you are a total person. People may get sick physically because of a mental or spiritual disturbance. Also it is tough to be your best mentally and spiritually if you are physically sick. So, watch your health closely. I am really going to give you some pointers on this in Part Three.

This world is exciting and yours to enjoy; and your body is the instrument through which the thrill of your physical existence comes to you. Your body is a wonderful instrument able to deliver to your senses the smell of a camp fire, the shock of cold water from your dive into the pool, and the terrific tastes of hamburger, pizza, and ice cream.

You should love yourself—because God made you. God did see fit to build this outstanding blend of muscle, bone, and brain into a body, the total of which is "you." God made it, so it is good.

You must appreciate self without being selfish

The Bible cautions us that we not "think of ourselves more highly than we ought." This means that we could go too far with our concentration on self and become an arrogant jerk. No doubt about it! We would not contribute either to our own happiness or the happiness of others by being self-centered, obnoxious snobs. No, we must think highly of ourselves, but not *only* of ourselves. Having this strong and positive feeling about ourselves as individuals of great value, we will be more likely to allow our appreciation of self to guide us to seek opportunities of service to others. This is God's plan. The right appreciation of self sets the stage for a life of service.

5

The World Is Yours—Reach Out and Take It

I grew up in South Texas near the King Ranch, the largest ranch in the United States. There's no hunting allowed on the King Ranch, so it is a huge game preserve. Many times I have hunted on adjoining ranches and have looked across the fence at this vast wilderness of woods and water with wild game still as plentiful as it must have been in pre-civilized America. At times like this, I understand why the Indians fought for their hunting grounds.

King Ranch has drawn me like a magnet; but the signs on those beautiful fences say, "no trespassing!" And they have fence riders to back up those signs, turning guys like you and me back to less fertile hunting grounds.

It really leaves me feeling rejected to think of all that fine hunting that I don't have the freedom to enjoy. But when I think about it, I realize that I couldn't have the freedom I have if other people weren't allowed to keep me off their property.

You live in a land of many freedoms

To say that the world is yours to enjoy isn't to deny the right of private ownership. You are guaranteed by this right to own private possessions. But you can enjoy the larger world in which you are free to live, explore, and mature, without violating anyone's rights.

You are very fortunate to live in a country where your rights as a free individual are protected by law. But even in countries where people are oppressed and denied their civil rights, some are able to be happy by exercising the freedom of the mind and spirit, even when physical liberties are denied. How fortunate you are to live in a land where you have so great a freedom!

The world was made for you

This world was designed especially for you, and you were designed to receive maximum benefits from your world. It is evident that in the entire creation event God had man in mind. He created the world and then made man, building into him the capabilities of enjoying and using the world He created.

What purpose would a watermelon have if God hadn't created your tongue to enjoy it? You should constantly remind yourself that the world is yours. It was meant for you. The Master Architect built the world first; but He already knew the kind of creature He would build to enjoy it.

You don't have to earn your right to happiness

You don't need to feel apologetic about being here in the world, because you are here according to God's plan. But every person who does not live fruitfully and happily fouls up his life, and in a way he is making God's creation a waste. Keep in mind that you don't have to win the privilege of being in the world, you are here because you have *already* found favor with God. And as a young Christian you have already acknowledged the gifts of God, including that supreme gift of His Son.

It really bothers me that some of you say you know these truths and still don't reach out and receive the benefits that God has already provided. I feel like saying "Wake up! Get with it!" It is almost impossible to understand how a person who knows these things could keep from being happy and excited.

It is hard to believe that thousands of people are letting life pass them by because they feel unworthy and downcast, filled with guilt feelings, and are not free to live joyously. They act like little children who see the beautiful toys through the shop window, but must deny themselves the pleasures of them because they belong to someone else. Happiness belongs to you just as much as to anyone else.

Don't let your background interfere with your happiness

It is possible that you have had some bad experiences which are making it difficult for you to have an optimistic view of life. Perhaps your home life was not what it might have been. Maybe you have been made to feel unworthy and unwanted by having experienced some discouraging comparisons with older brothers or sisters. Your early childhood experiences do have the power to weight you down and make it difficult to face the world and expect to win. A child who has been reared in a home where everyone has always looked at the bad side often sees things in the same manner for the rest of his life. Even the luckiest of us have probably had some really bad problems and experiences that have weakened our zest for life. We are creatures of habit, and it takes a special effort to break a habit.

But you are still young and flexible. As you get older, if you continue to have a pessimistic attitude, it will be harder to change. You must change now while you are still flexible. And you can!

Being creatures of habit, you can change a bad habit for a good one. You must begin right now to start thinking positively. This is your world, and it's up to you whether or not you take advantage of it. It's your choice. You can drag through life half-alive or you can arouse yourself and reach out and take the gifts of God. And if you do, you can expect a full and happy life.

So, make up your mind. It may not be easy and you may find yourself slipping backward into the old way of seeing things. You must replace the thoughts of failure with the thoughts of success. Believe me, thinking success can help you be successful.

I feel that God intended that everyone of us, in whatever we seek to do, be our very best and use this to His glory. We can only accomplish this when we are willing to discipline our imagination. And just as weight lifting is important to develop your body physically, so the psychological discipline of seeing yourself doing your job and doing your job well is necessary to discipline yourself psychologically. Napoleon said, "Imagination rules the world." Napoleon was right.

In a recent survey, reported in Dr. Maxwell Maltz's book *Psycho-Cybernetics,* twenty Physical Ed students were asked to shoot free throws on the basketball court. They practiced twenty minutes a day for twenty days. They improved twenty-four percent. Twenty other P.E. students simply sat in a room and *imagined* themselves shooting free throws. They imagined themselves stepping up to the free throw line. They imagined themselves taking the ball in hand. They imagined themselves firing the ball through the air and dropping it through the hoop. At the end of twenty days of twenty minutes of imagined practice per day they had the same rate of improvement as the ones who actually shot free throws. Isn't that amazing?

Is this to say that we can quit practicing and simply sit in an air-conditioned room and imagine ourselves practicing? Well, I know a lot of you lazy hound dogs would like to think it said that; and, in fact, it might—except for the fact that we wouldn't be in very good shape. Experiences vividly imagined have the same impact on your subconscious as experiences you actually live. Your nervous system can't tell the difference between a real experience and a vividly imagined experience, so your subconscious is either working for you or against you. If you see yourself as a social dud, you will be. If you see yourself as being a dud in business, you will be. You'll figure out a way to fail every time. If ever your imagination and your will power come into conflict, your imagination most likely will win.

Be glad for your own joys—never envious of others

You may be thinking that the other guys are a lot better off than you are. This is a "chicken way" to look at it. Sure, some people may have a lot of things you don't have. Some are highly intelligent, wealthy, physically attractive, etc., and maybe they're superior to you in some ways.

But there's one thing they are not—they are not *you*. No other person can make that claim. It's better to be you than to have all of these traits you admire in your friends. Be glad that they have these strong points and be glad that you are physically, mentally, and spiritually just who you are. You have a lot to be proud of. Yourself. Don't sell yourself short! You have no excuse for failing to live an abundant life. True, you may not have as much of an opportunity for success as some of your friends; but then, maybe you have some strengths they don't have.

A lot of you guys aren't even worth the ground upon which you stand, because you're not fulfilling the purpose for which you were created. And one of the reasons you're not doing it is because you're always trying to be something you're not. You're not what you're supposed to be. You're always looking at the other fellow wishing you could be like he is. I'll tell you guys something—I wouldn't be Billy Graham, Lyndon B. Johnson, or Johnny Unitas, even if I could be. It's okay by me just to be Bill Glass. And if you wish you could be your hero, all I can say is that there has to be a time when you quit hero worshipping and decide what *you* are meant to be.

Life is a big group of challenges

How do you know that any other person sees the same array of colors you see when you look at the sunset? How do you know how the soft spring breeze feels on the cheek of the other fellow? The other fellow doesn't know what he is missing in not being you, and only you can really appreciate your individual joys achieved as you live in this magnificent universe—your world.

Let me challenge you. Live in your world and be happy. Challenges are all around you. The fact that you have muscles in your body should challenge you to develop them. The existence of others should challenge you to develop friends. The thought of an opponent should challenge you to winning.

PART TWO

You Can Develop A Dynamic Personality

6

Be Your Best

In a game against the New York Giants, one of our backs gained 232 yards. What a day he had! Some backs would settle for that much yardage in a whole year.

I asked him, "Tell me how in the world did you do this? How did you get yourself ready to play this fantastic game?" He said, "Bill, you wouldn't believe me if I told you." I said, "Try me."

He said in explanation. "I sat day after day before that game in my room, in my car, wherever I was. I saw myself, I pictured myself, I visualized myself doing my job. I would see myself running out around end. I would see myself taking the ball from the quarterback and cutting in and out of blockers, around tacklers and through tacklers, and finally scoring. I would see myself as I ran off tackle and off guard, and I would see myself catching the ball. I saw myself in my imagination time after time after time. Then, when the actual game came up, to my amazement it happened just exactly as I had visualized it would. It was so vivid that it was just like a stage play."

I have to admit that in preparation for the games I've played in pro football for several years now, I've been using this technique. I see myself down on the line of scrimmage; I see myself fire across the line and hit into my opponent. I see myself pulling my opponent to the inside, charging to the outside, and rushing the passer. I see myself throwing Bart Starr for a ten yard loss. (I have to do it in imagination; it so seldom happens in reality.)

But you see, when you get into the game and it actually happens, that's not the first time it has happened. It happened a lot of other times in your imagination. Too many of you take a parachute with you into everything you do. You say, "Oh, I'm not going to do very well in this particular job, in this class, in this social situation, or in this game." And sure enough when you do fail in the game you've already got your parachute on and you're ready to bail out. And when, in fact, you don't do very well you say, "Just as I thought." Then you bail out. You've already made provision for your failure. You've preconditioned yourself to fail before you start. I say it would be infinitely better if you were to throw away your parachute and dive in with both feet and both hands.

You have become what you are because of the influences which have surrounded you since birth. "I don't like my personality," you say. Then why don't you improve it? If your personality has flaws you would like to correct, start changing now!

Now is the time to start

While you are still a young person, you have the ability to change your personality. As you grow older, though, you're going to have a bigger problem in changing. Why not take advantage of your youth?

The process of building a good personality probably involves only a partial change from your present way of doing things. You will need to develop only a few good traits you do not now have. Actually, you need to drop a few traits and add a few. Right now you probably have just about everything it takes to make a good personality—you just need to upgrade the qualities you have a little. Maybe your personality is a little rusty.

It's going to be necessary to set up some goals for your life in the future years, so you can build your personality to fit your needs. For example, if you're going to be a lawyer, you'll have to develop the ability to speak fluently to the public and in the courtroom. You will need to be friendly but persuasive, and you'll need to become suave socially. If you want to be a doctor, you'll have to develop confidence in your work, the type of attitude that draws patients, and a real appreciation of the art of medicine. If you want to be a bookkeeper, you will need to develop patience, neatness, and an ability to deal with figures. If you want to be a pro athlete, you'll have to be self-disciplined so you can concentrate and think on your feet.

But there are certain qualities everybody needs. No matter what you end up doing, you must have these qualities. For example, everybody has to get along with others, and everybody needs a friendly disposition.

Personality building is a process

It's not likely you'll be able to just decide to change yourself drastically and "presto" it's all done. Changing your personality is a difficult and an impossible thing unless you really try hard and constantly. The main difficulty will be keeping yourself content with your small daily gains which will soon create a massive gap between the old you and the new you. Many times you'll fail to make the goals and resolutions, but these shortcomings must make you even more determined to press toward the goals you have set for yourself. You've got to stand right up to the opposition and show everybody what kind of guts you have.

Get a picture in your mind of what you want to be

Get a picture in your mind of that best self you want to become. Most people select a person, real or fictional, that they want to be like. This isn't bad. Choose an ideal person and try to copy him. Certainly Christ is the ideal for every Christian, but a present-day ideal is good, too.

It really shakes me up to find that a certain guy uses me for an ideal. But you never really know when there is someone looking at you and reading your life like a book.

Let me show you what I mean with the following letter I received a few days ago:

> Dear Bill:
>
> I would like to tell you how much I admire you and the work you are doing. Most people think of a big hard knocking player like yourself as being a rough someone who goes out every night and gets drunk.
>
> I saw you play this year down in Atlanta, and there's one thing I would like to know—what were you saying to Randy Johnson after you lowered the boom on him? I sure felt sorry for Randy. But to see you lie on the ground with him and pat him on the back did me worlds of good and the people around me.
>
> After playing four sports in high school and trying to live a Christian life as I do, it's mighty nice to be able to say, "That Bill Glass is an All-Pro End and a good Christian man. . . ."

Don't be surprised if you find some neighborhood kid is idolizing you the same way. No, we can't be worthy of such admiration, but it is a challenge. The guy you don't want to let down most of all is *you.*

The only drawback to patterning yourself after an ideal is the fact that you would not really wish to be the *exact* replica of any person you may know. However, you can train yourself to be somewhat like that person, choosing to copy his most admirable traits.

It is really a mistake to place any person too high on a pedestal. Those you look up to are likely to have many weaknesses as well as good qualities. You will not be perfect either, and you should not expect to be, although you should always be moving in that direction.

You are human and you have human weaknesses

As you work toward the goals of personality you have set for yourself, you should remember that you are a human being. As such, you must recognize that you will occasionally do things and have feelings of which you may not be proud. When you cannot live up to your own goals, you must remember that God does not accept you because you do or do not reach your goals. His love is unconditional.

Human beings are probably the only creatures with the possibility for self-improvement. You cannot always become what you want to become, because some goals may be out of reach for you and some things are just not meant to be. On the other hand, you never get anywhere unless you make a genuine effort. The first step toward a better personality has to be developing a picture in your mind and heart of what you wish to become. Knowing what you want, and really wanting it with all your heart is more than half the battle. Don't let yourself think failure. If you allow yourself to think about the possibility of losing the game, you are much more likely to lose.

People live their lives by images. A lot of people have a "victim" image of themselves. They think they are simply victims of their circumstances. A lot of people have a second-string image of themselves; they don't really believe that they are quite first-stringers. A lot of people have the image of themselves being *real* men; they believe they have to be heavy drinkers, and immoral in their sex life. If you have that image, you probably got it from the movies or TV. Believe me, it's a deceptive image, and I know you have too much sense to continue to fall for it.

Dream, but dream sensibly

You must face up to whatever limitations you have. If you weigh one hundred-forty pounds, you can't expect to be a tackle with the

Cleveland Browns. You may dream all you like, but if you do it will just be a big waste.

Use your common sense; you're stupid if you don't. But dream big! Most of you are much too practical. You don't think big enough; you set goals that are much too small.

God gave you a mind to help you know what the realities are that you must face, but he also gave you an ambition to push you toward your highest level of achievement. Your job is to decide what is reasonable for you and what is within the will of God. So get with it, set a goal, and go for it!

7

Believe In Yourself

I remember when I made All-American my senior year at Baylor. I went on a trip to New York City to appear on the Ed Sullivan Show. I really enjoyed meeting those players from all over America who were supposedly the best that year.

But the one thing that was most surprising to me was their overpowering confidence. In fact, at the time I thought they were arrogant rather than confident. Many of them openly told me how great they were. I certainly felt confidence in myself but didn't feel it necessary to tell other people about it.

Well, the fact is, they *were* good. Most of them went on to be very fine pro football players. But I still feel that a guy ought to let others discover his greatness through watching his performance, not from his own bragging. I must admit that if you have to choose between confidence with bragging and insecurity without bragging, I'd choose the first every time.

Everyone benefits from self-confidence—the student, the athlete, the salesman, the politician. If you don't believe in yourself, you've had it before you even start.

You can do almost anything you think you can. And the guy who constantly beats his own efforts by not believing in himself will always be a loser. If you have real self-confidence, you will try harder and won't give up without a real fight.

You may have the idea that degrading yourself is humility. You say, "Oh, I can't do that," or "I'm not very good at that." You think you're very humble and that people will like you better because of it.

If I say to a player after the game, "You played a great game" and he says, "Ah, no I didn't do very well," he's verbally kicking himself in the seat of his pants. That's not humility. And if you make yourself believe your lies, it will destroy your self-confidence. Actually, you should be so wrapped up in what you're doing that you don't think of yourself so much as you think of getting to the goal. Then the self is not so important, and the goal is what is important. At the same time, you can't afford to forget self totally—that might affect your confidence.

To be self-confident you must know yourself

When you demand too much of yourself, you are likely to come out the loser. Obviously, you must know yourself; you must know what you're capable of accomplishing. Only by truly knowing yourself will you be able to gain confidence in your ability to do the job. I have actually heard some guys say, "The reason that I'm not popular is because I'm a Christian." I sometimes feel like saying, "It could be the reason you're not popular is because of your rotten personality." You know, you can't blame everything on God; it just could be that He intended for you to be as friendly and courteous and as popular as you possibly could be.

To be self-confident you must like yourself

You have confidence only in people you like—so don't expect to develop self-confidence unless you really like what *you* are. If *you* believe in *yourself,* you have won half the battle; the other half involves applying yourself to be the best you are capable of becoming.

Take the game of golf, for instance. If you really have some natural ability, and if you believe in yourself, you can be a champion. But you can't really be confident about your game unless you can shoot a relatively low score. And the only way you can make a low score is to learn the proper techniques and then practice until you are good enough. If you don't practice, you can't expect to do well, and if you don't do well you can't hope to have confidence. Even the professional golfers must develop their confidence in certain parts of their game over and over again. Having conquered problems with his putting, Arnold Palmer suggests a new type of practice for this most important part of the golf game. His practice consists of using a dime as a hole in his living room carpet. The object of the practice is to putt the ball from various distances, so that it stops directly on top of the dime. He says that doing this even once out of every hundred attempts helps build his confidence and improves his game. When he gets on the green in the championship tournament, that hole looks huge compared to the dime.

Many track men wear leg weights during practice in order to strengthen their legs. But more importantly, when they take the weights off for the big race, their legs feel light. Confidence is increased and they are able to do a great deal better. They are not really *physically* a lot faster or stronger; but they *feel* faster and stronger, and so they are. I have worn leg weights for the same reason. It does wonders for my confidence.

Success brings self-confidence

I know a lot of football players who come out for football in junior high school and high school because they think it is the thing to do. They do it because they think it will make them more popular, etc. But, they never really become confident, because they don't put themselves into it enough to become really good.

I remember when I first went out for football in junior high school. I tried to play quarterback. My brother had been a quarterback, and I thought that just because he played quarterback I could too. He had been All-State in high school football at quarterback and I thought I could too. But when I tried to play quarterback, rather than being All-State I was just "all wet." He was my idol and I wanted to follow in his footsteps.

I constantly got knocked flat of my back; and I remember at one point during the seventh grade, when I was trying to play quarterback during a scrimmage, two big linemen charged in, hit me, and knocked me for a loop. I really got clobbered and the field was kind of rough, so they scratched up my face. At that stage I didn't like football because I didn't have any self-confidence. I wasn't doing a good job at all. But I had to stay out there, because I was Vernon Glass' little brother. He was a great high school football player, and I had to do this as a status symbol. This continued all the way through junior high school and until my sophomore year in high school. I was simply forced to go out for football because of my older brother.

Then one day my uncle took me aside and told me that it was ridiculous for me not to be playing first string, because I was bigger than any of the rest of the guys, or at least a lot of them; and I should be able to tear those guys up and be a first-stringer. Well, the very next day in workout I hit that guard in front of me so hard that it knocked him flat of his back. I was more surprised than anyone, but I decided that this was the way to play football. As the days went by, and I continued to be more and more aggressive and to develop into a better and better football player, my confidence grew and I came to love the game more and more. When I graduated from high school, I was developing more agility and speed, I was learning to play the game better, and I was determined to be the best player I could.

The first four years I played football I didn't really enjoy it—in fact, I kind of hated it. But after that experience during my sophomore year in high school, I began to really like it; and by my senior year in high school I liked it very much. Then all the way through my college days, I grew to like it more and more because I was not only developing confidence but at the same time I was developing ability in the game. I suppose that I enjoy football as much as anything I have ever done, because now I have been playing organized football for twenty years—ten years as an amateur and ten years as a pro. The point is: that I developed confidence only after I started doing okay. So, you see, confidence depends on doing a good job and doing a good job depends on confidence. It's a two-way street.

It's bad enough to watch a guy strive for a goal that he hasn't the ability to reach. But, I really get frustrated when I see a boy who has everything it takes but who fails miserably because he is just flat lazy and hasn't the guts to bet on himself. If you are one of these guys, you are just going to have to make up your mind to use your abilities to the fullest—you must make a super effort. Nobody is going to blame you if you just haven't got it, but if you have it and don't get with it, everybody will be down on you. And you will be down on yourself. There are many who have been sharper that Helen Keller, but because she was deaf, dumb, and blind, when she wrote something it carried a lot of weight. She has supremely used her potential, so she is highly respected.

You've got to believe in yourself even when nobody else does

Remember, it's more important for you to believe in yourself than for someone else to believe in you. Sure, you have to be realistic about your abilities, but don't expect others to push you forward because *they* think you are capable. How are they going to know what you've got deep down inside—only you can know that!

It's a little hard for me to give credit to the opposition, but look at the Dallas Cowboys. Everyone knows this is one of the best teams in the country. But did you know that back in 1965 their entire starting defensive secondary signed with Dallas as "free agents?" This means that nobody wanted them in the draft. These guys believed in themselves, even though nobody else seemed to believe in them. That's what you are going to have to do many times in your life.

Track is the best example of this. Ten years ago they said, "No one can run a four-minute mile. It's humanly impossible." But now everybody that's anybody is running a four-minute mile. They said, "Nobody can vault over fifteen feet. The laws of gravity just won't let a man go that high in the air with nothing to help him but a skinny pole." But now everybody that's anybody is vaulting over seventeen feet. They also said, "No one can high jump over seven feet." But now several have, and the same is true of almost every event in track. Are people that much faster or stronger? No, I think that when one person breaks a so-called barrier, then people don't sabotage their own chances with a lack of belief.

Where does self-confidence come from?

Self-confidence comes from attempting those things you are capable of doing and of learning to do those things well. But this is only part of the story.

The ability to have a feeling of confidence also depends on the entire story of your life up to the present. Some people are never able to develop self-confidence, even for the most insignificant tasks.

You see, the feeling of confidence in the broadest possible sense comes from your positive reactions to successful experience reaching all the way back into your childhood years. If you don't seem to have confidence in yourself even for the things you know you are qualified to do, then it is very probable that you have developed a poor way of thinking which began during your early childhood.

Maybe you weren't allowed to do things for yourself when you were a child. Or maybe you have been unfavorably compared to brothers and sisters. You may feel inferior because an older sister, brother, or playmate was always better than you were.

There are all kinds of misfortunes of early childhood that could have caused you to lose confidence. For now, I couldn't care less about your past! It's too late to worry about that. The important thing is your future and what you are going to do to get yourself in shape for a great life. That's what really counts! You must get ready to make the most of everything you have—believe in what you are and what you can become.

You have plenty going for you

Now I realize that a lot of you may think you don't have a great deal to believe in. You're sort of like that guy back in high school whose name was Slick. Slick was so skinny that it was almost unbelievable. In fact, he was so skinny that if he ever turned sideways and stuck out his tongue, he'd look like a zipper. But one day, working out for basketball, Slick went in for a lay-up, but he went too far and went past the backboard, ran into the wall, and cut his leg pretty badly. He asked the coach if he could go into the dressing room and get some merthiolate to put on his leg. The coach agreed, so Slick went into the dressing room; and he came back out in just a little while with a merthiolate bottle in his hand.

Holding the bottle up high, he yelled across the court, "Coach," he said, "the glass dipper in the merthiolate bottle is broken off. How do I get the merthiolate out of the bottle and onto my leg?"

Now the coach didn't want to stop the work-outs to discuss a glass dipper in a merthiolate bottle with Slick, so he just yelled back over his shoulder, "Slick, take the bottle cap off and stick your leg in the bottle."

I admit that a lot of you think you don't have a great deal to believe in in the first place, but everyone of you has a great deal more than you could ever imagine. Everyone of you has fantastic capabilities, which if you would tap, you could be much, much more effective in whatever you do than you are. I mean that socially, intellectually, and athletically. Carlyle has said, "Alas, the most fearful unbelief is unbelief in yourself." A low opinion of yourself is not a virtue, it's a vice. The Scripture says, "Love your neighbor as yourself." But how can you love your neighbor, if you don't love yourself? I'm simply suggesting that you believe in yourself and realize that you're a creature created in the image of God and that you have innate worth.

You must have a healthy self-respect. You must believe that you are capable of attaining almost anything you set your mind on. If you continually kick yourself in the seat of the pants, you make it a lot less likely that you'll be successful in whatever you try to do. It would be infinitely better if you would believe in yourself and believe that you're capable of doing anything. Success breeds success.

Maybe some unthinking parent or teacher suggested to you when you were quite young that you weren't very effective in reading, and all your life you've been carrying this picture of yourself around in your mind of being a poor reader. No matter how hard you try you're going to figure a way to read poorly. The only way I know to get out of this is to constantly feed yourself pictures of yourself doing well in reading. As Fran Tarkenton says, "Carry the image of victory in your heart."

You can and you must overcome the bad in your past

Everyone is influenced by the past, but no one needs to be a victim of his past. With what God has given you, both physical and mental, you can rise above your past. You must decide that you will achieve your desires—desires based on reasonable goals which in turn are based on your own individual strengths and weaknesses.

No matter what problems you have encountered in the past, you can conquer these problems now. And in the future you must dare to move forward with strong determination. You must face life with courage. Start with little things and work up to the big.

It won't be easy, and you may slip at times. Take courage and try again when you fail to measure up to what you know you can do. You can't get anywhere without trying. And once you taste a little success, you will find the going much easier, just like I did that day in high school, when I really hit someone and found that it worked.

If you don't feel confident, act confidently

You are a creature of habit. You can consciously force yourself to do things that you usually don't do. If you do this long enough, it will begin to feel normal.

Even if you don't feel confident, act confidently. Your actions will be contagious and you will soon begin to feel confident. Smile and you will feel happier; talk louder if you are timid in a social group; walk boldly if you are afraid. See yourself in your imagination as the ideal person, and you will become just that.

You can't always win

Even the person with great self-confidence doesn't expect things to work out every time. You will need to develop the habit of taking failures in stride, looking for your mistakes, finding, and correcting them. You must hate to lose because good losers usually lose, but you can learn from mistakes and then forget them. No one expects perfection, and you must not expect it of yourself. And even when you succeed, you should remember that your performance might have been better.

You should study yourself, find your weaknesses, and improve with every experience. No matter how well I think I played in the game, on film day I usually discover it wasn't as good as I thought.

Don't be afraid to take reasonable chances

If you wait until you are absolutely sure of success, you will keep on waiting. We have an expression for this in pro football—"no guts, no glory." If you don't take a chance, you can't win. There is a gamble in everything you will do; and you will need to develop good judgment about everything.

I believe that everyone of us was born with natural desire to gamble. We're all born gamblers. But you see the way it was intended that we use this natural desire to gamble was that we gamble on ourselves and on our ability to attain what we go after. But a lot of people have perverted this natural desire to gamble to the gambling table or the race track. A lot of people are such cowards that they don't really have the guts to bet on themselves and so they bet on the gambling tables or on the race track. Sometimes you've got to throw away your parachute and dive in with both feet. Believe in yourself and have the guts to bet on yourself. But once you have decided to take that risk, really go all out to make things work out. And even if you don't quite make the grade, don't let it shake your self-confidence. You should believe in yourself so strongly that you are willing to take risks knowing that you can't always be lucky and come out with the ball bouncing in your favor. Sometimes things will go against you that you couldn't possibly foresee.

A really easy way to see the merits of a sensible gamble is seen in the actions of a man returning punts. Mike Garrett of Kansas City is a good example of a punt returner who seldom makes the fair catch. He always tries to field the ball and many times is able to take advantage of good blocking and his own great running to make extra yardage or six points, just because he had the guts to take a risk. But don't forget that sometimes he gets knocked silly and gains nothing but a headache. Yet he never hesitates to take the risk again. Never be afraid to gamble on yourself—just gamble intelligently.

If you have a strong fear that what you do will turn out wrong, you are sure to lose confidence. Just put your best into whatever you undertake; believe in yourself and you will win most of the time.

8

An Outgoing Personality Will Win for You

Fred likes to be with people, is always on the move, spends little time thinking of himself. He's a real extrovert. Tom is shy and withdrawn from society, keeping to himself, studying his own feelings. He's a real introvert. Some people are outgoing like Fred. Others are quiet and turned inward like Tom. People can be divided into two basic groups, the extroverts and the introverts.

Now, of course, you aren't likely to be either an extreme introvert or extrovert. Most of you are somewhere in between. If you are more of an introvert than an extrovert, that doesn't mean that life will pass you by or that you can't be a success. It does mean that you would be happier doing certain kinds of work where you can just be yourself. Remember, you don't *have* to become an extrovert to be happy.

The extrovert usually comes out ahead

However, you should stop and think. Who makes the biggest success? Isn't it the people with outgoing personalities who have the most success in making money, creating desirable influences, and being popular? Our culture is just built that way. The most successful people are usually the extroverts. It is also true that since your service to God must be a service to your fellow man, the extrovert has something of an advantage in *most* areas of Christian service. But don't be misled, the introverted scientist working alone in a laboratory could develop a drug which would mean more to the welfare of millions than the work of the most outgoing salesman, minister, or politician could possibly mean.

You ask, "Should I try to build an outgoing personality?" That all depends upon what you really want in life. A fair guess would be that most of you would be better off if you could be more congenial. It may be hard, but in most cases, at least a slight change is necessary.

Being shy is a quality that has been built into you since you were a little child. Shyness may be difficult to overcome unless you realize that it is largely a habit. Maybe you got into the habit of being shy because of childhood events; the habit may be something you just fell into without knowing how or when. No matter how you got that way, the answer is the same—a habit must be broken by substituting another habit in its place. In other words, in spite of what might have happened to you as a little child, you can now develop the habit of being an outgoing personality.

You can't throw out shyness by will power; you must replace it with boldness. Do it in little things at first. Start sitting on the front row and push yourself a little in social situations. Always add your "two bits" to every conversation. Don't be afraid to speak up.

You may have to push yourself

Some guys are never able to break out of the shell they've been in all their lives. And that is all right; they can be happy and successful, even if they are the quiet type. Maybe it will be the same for you.

But at least you should be willing to move toward a more outgoing personality, realizing that the best of everything seems to come to the outgoing person. If you wish to move up a notch or so toward a more outgoing person, you are going to have to work on some new habits. You are going to have to smile when you don't feel like smiling, look people full in the eye, and stretch out your hand in greeting when you feel like running away. These are the types of things extroverts do, so you must force yourself to do them. This will be sort of like breaking in a new glove. At first it feels different, but after you've got it broken in you like it much better than the old glove. You may feel funny at first, but soon this will become a way of life and be natural to you.

I have a friend named Fred Smith. He says when he was twenty-one he was sitting in the back of an auditorium, alone as usual. And he began to think, "All my life I've been a loner. I've been afraid to speak up. I've even skipped college because I'm so introverted."

But as he began to look around that audience at the people he knew, there wasn't one successful person there that wasn't an extrovert. The introverts he knew were the failures or just barely making it. So he said to himself, "If the extroverts are the successful people, I'll be an extrovert." He began to do everything the extroverts do. Today, Fred Smith is the biggest extrovert that I know and is an overwhelming success in every way.

Here is the important thing. By putting on a front, by acting like an extrovert even though it takes some effort, you will at least give yourself the opportunity of knowing whether or not you are going to like it. Give it a fair trial. Chances are that you are going to find a whole new world opening up for you, a world you didn't even know existed—a world of happy, friendly people.

But if you have to keep on faking, it isn't you

In the long run, you just can't keep on faking what you don't really feel, however. People will begin to know you for a phony and will not respond to you. That's the whole point —if you have to keep on faking, you should give it up as a bad job. On the other hand, if acting like an extrovert starts coming natural for you, then move right along with it, and continue to develop your outgoing qualities. It will be genuine because you will have come to know that all you really lacked in being a natural extrovert was the guts to try.

Friendliness is the natural way

By nature we were meant to be friendly and outgoing. You are supposed to like others, live happily with others, and serve one another. The Bible constantly teaches Christians to "bear ye one another's burdens." This idea of many people living together is accepted almost everywhere, and only the emotionally ill isolate themselves completely from others.

It is important to your success in life, whether you count success in terms of money you make or in terms of services you render, that you must reach out to other people. An important part of this outreach is your ability to know other people and to get them to know you.

Success comes to the young person who makes a real effort to know many people around about him by their names, their occupations, and associations. As a young person you should really try to learn the names of persons in your church, your neighborhood, and school. For instance, suppose there's a real sharp teacher in your high school or college whose name you don't know. It's up to you to learn it! One of these days you may run into him in the hallway. Look at him, smile and say, "Good morning, Mr. Knight." You can bet he'll smile back; and a few more little things like this will make him wonder what *your* name is.

Thus, because of your outgoing personality you have made a potential friend. You are alert to people, you feel warmly toward them, and while you're not primarily polishing the apple, it sure can't hurt a guy. These people you call by name will help you a lot quicker than if you didn't bother with it. If you think you don't need people, you are flat wrong.

Make it a habit to see the best in others

People are important to you. In order to develop a good outgoing personality, you must believe that people are basically good. You must develop the ability to see the best in others. Unless you do, you will not be able to respond warmly to them. Unless you are able to see the good points in everyone you meet and place more value on those points, you will be a phony in your efforts to be warm and friendly.

Remember, there are all kinds of people, some with values like yours and some with ideas quite different from yours. In some instances, you may want to try to help others change their values; but even in this matter, the point of communication with them is to let them see that you accept them as persons of great worth and value, no matter how different they may be. I notice that Jesus was a lot more comfortable with pagans than most Christians are, and yet he was perfect. There will be times that you'll be with people who are miles from you in their convictions. You must allow them this freedom.

Don't withdraw, infiltrate

As you develop your outgoing personality, you will find that you *naturally* want to be with people. You will become a joiner; you will be active in all kinds of projects. Joining worthwhile groups is a means of growing up with a good personality. Just be sure the groups you join have high ideals and purposes, and be sensible about the number you join. You don't want to spread yourself too thin. Grab every opportunity to move out among people. The more people you know and who know you, the fuller your life will be.

In this as with all things, some moderation must be applied. Choose your friends wisely, leaving plenty of time to study, work, and do all the things you want for a full life. Don't miss knowing people; they can be enjoyable.

Learn to hold your head high, to look your fellow human beings in the eye, and to move with finesse among people of all types and all walks of life. This is the way Christ did it. He was everybody's friend.

9

You Should Have Class

In the NFL, it's written into our contracts that we agree to wear a suit and tie in all public appearances when representing our club. But there is a fierce pride that develops on a team so that if a player isn't dressed right, he is ribbed until he does shape-up to meet the highest standards in his appearance.

The pressure from the contract is nothing compared to the pressure that comes when an old vet says to a rookie, "Rook, you keep wearing these clothes and they'll come back into style in a few years." Or when the vet says, "Let's pass the hat and buy this poor rookie an overcoat."

Even when another veteran wears something that's a little below the standard, it's commented on in a good natured way. He usually doesn't make the mistake the second time.

If you are going to be an outstanding Christian, you must think of yourself as having "class." You're the best this world has to offer. There is no one more worthwhile than you; no one is superior to a young man who has made Christ an example and Lord of his life.

It doesn't matter if your folks aren't the greatest or the richest. People recognize class when they see it; and you must take pride in being just who you are if you want to have class. Some may have better clothes than you, but no one should be able to stand straighter or be prouder to be a man.

Show the world you are a thoroughbred

A healthy pride in yourself always shows through. You must be alert to the things that put you out front. You are a representative of so many things that you can't afford to ignore your impact on other people. You represent Christ, and that is the most important thing in the world. You also represent your parents and your family. Everyone who sees you relates you to the other members of your family. A family is known by the young men and women it produces. And remember, try to look sharp because your appearance is "you" to the world. You can't afford to be careless about it.

There's something about the way a thoroughbred horse handles himself that shows his breeding. It's the way he holds his head, the way he walks, his sleek appearance. Everyone who sees him says, "Now, there's a real thoroughbred." The same thing is true of you; the way you look, walk, and talk will mark you as a thoroughbred or a second-rate jerk.

Watch your grooming

Grooming is important. There was a time, when you were younger, that you could wear sloppy jeans, go around with messy hair, and get by with it; but not now. Now you are becoming a man and people expect much more of you. Remember everything about you must reflect class—not conceit, but class.

You can judge your quality of grooming by checking on a few important things. Do you bathe often and use plenty of deodorant? Do you brush your teeth at least twice a day and use a good mouth wash? Remember, body odor and bad breath are highly offensive.

You can't afford to be too different from your gang, but you can follow the lead of the best dressed boys in your group. And even though you may have to stick with the crowd as to the *style* of your clothes, there is usually no pressure forcing you to be *sloppy* in your clothes. Blue jeans or slacks can be clean and pressed; they can fit and can be worn so that they are good looking. It isn't so much *what* you wear as the *condition* of your clothes and the *way* you wear them.

Your shoes probably show up more than anything you wear. Keep them clean, in good condition, and shining. Look them over every time you leave your room, have your shoe shine kit handy, and use it often.

Girls are real careful about their hair. Too often boys couldn't care less. But it's a fact that a man's hair and the way he keeps it is the chief indicator of what he thinks of himself. Keep it cut, clean, and styled; but not in the way-out styles that say to the world, "Here comes a rebel." I use a styling gel for men. It's really great, because it keeps my very unruly hair in shape and is not greasy.

A good well-balanced life depends on being accepted by older people as well as by friends. You need the acceptance of the majority more than the rebel group.

If you wish to call attention to yourself, you can do so by sloppy dress and way-out hair styles; but a better way is really good grooming. Dressing sloppily will cause you to be left out by the people who really count. The neatness shows the world that you are a man of pride—a person proud to be a man.

You remember that in an earlier chapter I had a lot to say about being yourself. That's really important, but I wouldn't want you to make the big mistake that some guys often make.

Some of you may think that being yourself means being sloppy—just letting go. Well, let me tell you that being sloppy is a poor excuse for being yourself. Sure, you may want to put on some old clothes and go out in the country, do a little fishing, hunting, and so on. This kind of letting down is really good for you. But sloppy dress as a way of life is something else again. You must be yourself, but be your best self; and don't use "being yourself" to excuse your laziness. I can't believe that is the real you, and if suggesting that you be yourself means that you start looking like a "hood," then remember I also said, "Be your best self." The "hood" is usually miserable because he doesn't have a satisfactory goal for his life. If he doesn't know it already, he'll find out sooner or later. You want to be yourself, but even more than that you want to have a goal and the guts to get there.

Your face is your most important physical feature

You know, of course, that one of the marks of a man is a clean shaven face, free of pimples and skin blemishes. You're probably having some skin problems. If so, you should watch your diet, cutting way down on fats; and you should get a good antiseptic soap and use it often.

When I was your age, I had real problems with my skin. No one took the time to help me until I already had a pretty bad case of acne. It took me a long time to get rid of it. I wish someone had told me as I'm telling you, to see a doctor! Diet and cleanliness do the job most of the time, but don't hesitate to go to a dermatologist (skin specialist) if you continue to have trouble.

As soon as your beard starts to grow, shave every day. In your early manhood, you may feel that every other day or twice a week is enough, but the every-morning shave will do a great deal to stimulate your skin, and help to avoid pimples; and if you use a razor blade, it will give you a good opportunity to wash your face thoroughly. Nothing robs a guy of the healthy feeling of being a man like having a pimply face.

Good manners are the mark of a gentleman

If you have taken the time and effort to make yourself look as sharp as possible, then you shouldn't stop there. The better you look to people, the more closely they watch you; and I know you don't want to ruin your first good impression by failing to act as good as you look.

Being a man with real class is your goal. There are certain things that are expected of you. The only way to excel in this is to study what is expected and to follow through. Manners are for the most part common sense. It is not difficult to know how to act in most situations; just do what is logically right. Good etiquette isn't hard if you are just willing to try a little bit.

A large portion of your manners involve the way in which you treat women. If you want to be known as a top-flight person, then watch your conduct with the ladies. Show them every reasonable courtesy—never sit when they are standing, offer them support in difficult situations, open doors for them, and walk so as to offer them the best protection from traffic and crowds. In short, be attentive to the ladies, both young and old. It's a good thing to start with your mother and sisters.

The way you eat in public is another part of etiquette. Get a good book on table manners, observe and practice all the rules. Remember, in a public gathering, the way you eat is more important than your appetite. Good manners will help you socially more than you could ever imagine; and bad manners will make you go over like a lead balloon. The best place to practice is in your home. Remember, you *play* like you *practice*. You can't expect to have good public manners if you slurp, smack, and chew with your mouth open when you are at home.

Your public image and how you see yourself are both important

You must practice seeing yourself as a successful man, ready for any situation, but you shouldn't become conceited. You won't, if you remember that as important as you are, God has made you to serve as a little cog in His mighty army here on this earth. However, you can accomplish your part of His plan only if you maintain a high self-image, a healthy self-esteem.

People will see you basically as you see yourself. If you see yourself as a person of such importance that nothing and no one else matters, other people will see you as an obnoxious snob. You do have to seek a happy medium here, as in all things. You must have a healthy self-esteem and with it a great desire for service to others.

Take some time for yourself just to be yourself

There is a certain amount of pressure that comes from being with people no matter how friendly you may be by nature. You shouldn't neglect getting off to yourself from time to time, just to relax. Many busy businessmen take off a week or so in the fall to go hunting in the wilds. There they don't shave for a week, and in general relax from all the social duties of our highly complex modern life. This is a healthy thing to do, occasionally.

The fact that you like to get away from it all for a little while doesn't mean that you don't enjoy being with people. It's only that after a break like this you can return to enjoy them even more.

As a young man, you would probably find it wiser to take just a little time now and then to get out and rough it for an afternoon with a pal, or maybe your dad, if you enjoy being with him. You will come back refreshed and at peace with the world.

PART THREE

How To Build A Healthy and Powerful Body

10

Physical Fitness Is a Must for Every Christian

You need a powerful body even if you're not going to be a professional athlete

Most people picture the Christian as a person of meekness and gentleness. Some seem to picture Christ as an anemic, weak, spineless sort of person. Don't you believe it!

It is true that Christ indicated in several places in the Scriptures that the body is less important than the soul, and this has caused a great many people to get the wrong idea. But don't forget that the Scriptures also refer to the body as "the temple of the soul."

Physical fitness and the Christian life definitely go hand in hand. How can you possibly be all you should be for God in service if you aren't physically fit?

Back in 1964, Billy Graham began a plan of physical fitness for himself that he follows every day of the week including Sunday. He found that he was much stronger and could be a powerhouse for God, only if he maintained his physical body at a peak of fitness.

Many of you guys want to be athletes, professional or otherwise.

If so, you've got to really think about body building. But it is a mistake to think that you have an obligation to God and yourself to build a powerful body *only* if you are going to be an athlete. Actually, the same rules of health and physical fitness apply to everyone.

Play every sport that you really enjoy

A good friend of mine, Vince Costello, who played middle linebacker for us for many years at Cleveland told me one day, "I think the best thing for a boy who wants to be a pro football player is to play, play, play." By this he means that you should just play for the sheer joy of playing.

Play every sport that you really enjoy. Vince has a camp for boys in Ohio; and believe me they play every sport possible and have a really great time. Now, of course, he's speaking primarily of grade school and junior high school boys. But even in high school, college, and pro athletics there is much to be said for participating in many different sports. Even if your prime goal is football, there are other sports that are great, such as basketball and handball, which are very good in helping football players to become agile.

Suppose you were to ask a real good high school athlete, "Say, buddy, what sport do you like best?" If he's in football season, he'll say, "football." If he's in baseball season, he'll say, "baseball." If it's during basketball season, he'll say, "basketball," and if it's in early springtime, he'll say, "track." He likes the sport that he happens to be participating in at the time. And this is not bad—in fact, it is very good, because it is good for an athlete to have diversification, particularly when he is young.

Just as you wouldn't ask a future insurance salesman to settle down and start selling insurance when he is in high school, neither would you expect a future pro to settle down to just those things which would help him to become a great pro football player. In fact, it could be that participating in the different sports would actually help him in the long run to be a better football player, because he would be more eager both psychologically and physically.

Your weaknesses might become strengths

Fifteen or twenty years ago when an athlete had a weakness—for example, say he was weak in the arms even though he might have had strong back and legs, the coach would say, "Well, he has weak arms," and let it go at that. Now we can actually do something about it. We can say, "Let's put him on the weights and build his arms up so they are just as strong as the rest of his body." If a player is weak in blocking, we work on his blocking. He might be strong as a runner, strong as a passer, and strong as a receiver; but he needs to learn how to block, so we work on his blocking.

When you are involved in all of these other sports, if there is some area in which you see a weakness, that is the area in which you should work hardest. If you have weak arms for football, they would also bother you in baseball. Therefore, you should work on certain weight training exercises. But this shouldn't be done until you become burned out on weight lifting. This shouldn't take away from the enjoyment of the different sports, in fact it should add to it. As you become more proficient, you also enjoy it more.

My brother Vernon said that when he was in high school, he overheard one coach say to another, "We can't run Glass on that end sweep, because he's too slow." But the track coach, Smiley Davis told him, "That's just a bunch of bull. Glass can learn to run a lot faster." The coach said to Vernon, "Why don't you come out for track?"

Vernon protested, saying, "I'm not fast enough to run track." The coach said, "That's all right; you come out for track and get with my dash men until you get fast." So he did, and the next year he was running the end sweeps as well or better than anyone else.

Out in Palo Alto, California, Paul Wiggin and Monte Clark of the Cleveland Browns work out with Floyd Peters of the Philadelphia Eagles. They lift weights for about forty-five minutes and then play basketball for an hour. They do this every other day throughout most of the off season. There is nothing in their workouts that is distinctly football, but almost everything they do is helpful to them in football.

Ronnie Goodwin of the Philadelphia Eagles and I play handball and lift weights together here in Waco. Handball, like basketball, teaches the low, quick movements.

A lot of the pro football teams have formed little player-managed basketball teams. A bunch of the Browns play semi-pro basketball games all over a three-state area around Cleveland. Vince Costello books the team and handles all the arrangements. They average playing about three times a week for the off season. They usually play some local team. Any way you look at it, basketball is the most popular off season conditioner for pro football players. Golf may run a close second. The only problem with golf is that it takes so much time, and doesn't give you a good enough workout.

But let's suppose you are a high school junior or senior, and you want a little more complete instructions than "play, play, play." I certainly realize that not all of you want to play pro football. In fact, some of you don't care about coming out for sports at all. But you do realize that every Christian must be the best and most fully developed person he can be, morally, spiritually, and physically. As the Scriptures say, you are seeking to attain "to mature manhood, to the measure of the stature of the fullness of Christ."

You are dedicated—you've set yourself some goals and you mean business. This section of the book is definitely for *you!*

11

First You Must Tone-Up and Get In Shape

Right now I am going to tell you how you can take that body of yours and make a powerhouse out of it. It doesn't matter whether you are skinny or fat; either way, you can start from where you are and build a beautiful body that will be a source of pride and motivation for you and will make you gain self-confidence. If you are flabby physically, it can affect you mentally and spiritually. It helps your influence for Christ when you are in shape physically.

There are three things involved in having a powerful body. They are exercise, diet, and good habits. In this and the following two chapters, we are going to deal with exercise. You can tear your body down with exercises. You can build it up with exercise—it all depends on how you go about it. You can take off fat and put on muscle at the same time.

Get your body ready for the heavier stuff

I am going to level with you. Exercise will build a body that you can be proud of; but there are only a few people who have the "stickability" to make it come true. The secret isn't so much in the exercises I am going to give you as in your determination to follow-through with them. Exercises won't do you one bit of good if they stay as printed matter on the pages of this book—reading about them will only make you disgusted with the body you have. I can guarantee that if you do what I tell you, you will have a tremendous increase in strength, in body size, shape, and condition. Muscles will bulge all over you. This is what we call "definition," meaning that rather than muscles being embedded in baby fat, they become clearly defined so that you can see them even on the surface. But you can't expect this to happen unless you really get with it and stay with it. It'll take as much "stickability" as anything you ever did. Some of you guys are pretty soft because you've been living the soft life—sitting in front of the TV, eating too many sweets; the fastest you ever move is to get to the table, and the heaviest weight you lift is the keys to your car. All of this will have to stop, at least as a way of life. To be strong and healthy, you've got to live life with zest—get some pep into you, or as one of our coaches says, "Get the lead out!" You know what you want, but it won't come to you without great effort on your part.

To have a strong body, you've got to want it badly enough to sacrifice to get it. You should begin to change your self-image by seeing yourself in your imagination as you want to become. See the huge shoulders, the big biceps, the well-developed legs. Imagine the reactions of your girl friend, teammates, parents, and teachers. This motivation must change to a *burning desire,* if you are to have a great body.

You must learn to breathe properly

The source of life is oxygen which can nourish your body and cause it to develop, only if it gets into your lungs. Many people don't even know how to breathe—they've never really filled their lungs with the fresh air that's all around them.

Before you start on tone-up exercises, you should learn to breathe. You breathe about twenty-one times a minute. It is an automatic response; but you can develop the habit of breathing deeply, of getting the maximum of oxygen into your system—without plenty of oxygen, your muscles will never grow.

You shouldn't rush uncoached into a heavy set of exercises. You've got to take it gradually and build up to the heavier stuff. Many of you guys get on a body-building binge, grab a bunch of weights, and start pushing them around. This is really dangerous because you could strain yourself or hurt your back. You must build up very slowly. Then by the time you progress to the heavy weights you're in shape for it.

So, let's start with breathing. Get and keep clean workout clothes, including socks, jockstrap, tennis shoes, shorts, and tee shirt. Find a well-ventilated place to workout and follow this routine. Stand flat-footed and exhale every bit of the stale air out of your lungs—all of it. Do this with your arms loosely at your sides. Then as you start to inhale, raise your arms gradually as you suck the air in, way in. Let your chest expand, push the air deep down inside you, making your diaphragm expand. Pull in all you can, raising your arms as high as they'll go. Get on tiptoe to pull in that last bit of air.

Now, with arms descending slowly and coming down off your toes, exhale. Get rid of all of it, letting your shoulders droop, cross your arms and squeeze out the last bit of stale air. Now you have completed the cycle.

Start your morning with these breathing exercises. Get that oxygen into your system. Start out with about a dozen of these cycles, being careful not to overdo it at first. If you get dizzy, stop until the next workout. Then do another series just before bedtime. The whole idea is to get you to develop the habit of breathing deeply all day long. You see, your food gets to your body through your blood stream just as oxygen does. Breathing is the basis of all body building, because without it your muscles can't be properly nourished, no matter how much you eat or exercise.

You need to do some running and walking

The basic exercise of all athletes is walking and running. You can't get in shape without both. When we come to training camp in mid-July, we have to be in shape when we get there. The players use different routines of getting in shape. They all start light and build up slowly. Some use the routine the club suggests, and some have their own ideas of what's best for them. Some do very little off-season training in running or on the weights. Boy, can you tell the difference between the ones who do and the ones who don't. The great majority are in good shape when they come to training camp.

The most disgusting thing in the world is to see a rookie come to camp out of shape and overweight. Many times they throw away their chance in this way. Maybe they wouldn't make it anyway, but they'll never know, because they weren't in good enough shape to be able to tell.

Below you will find a conditioning schedule that I have borrowed from the Philadelphia Eagles. Every pro team has a routine that they suggest their players use to get in shape during the off-season. Now, this one may be too strenuous for you, so I am going to figure you are smart enough to cut it down to size. After all, I don't know how old you are or what shape you're in when you start. You do have to start off easy, because even at best you are going to be really sore for awhile. If you get too sore, it slows down your progress; when you start too fast, you get sore and don't stick with it. But you are going to have to stick with it, and the soreness will vanish. This is an eight week schedule, as you can see.

If your coach gives you an exercise routine to get you in shape before the season starts, use it. If you are not out for a sport, you can use these. You might show this plan to your coach and see what he thinks. But above all, do what your coach tells you and go beyond that only if he says okay. Remember, you can tear down as well as build up.

If you aren't out for a sport but only want to build your body, you will not have to go full force on the running part. But I do want you to get in enough running to get those legs in shape, get your wind built up, and your body thoroughly toned. I want you to get in shape *before* you start out with the other exercise plan I am giving you, *whether or not you are out for a sport.*

Philadelphia Eagles Eight Week Running Program—Five Day Week

Mr. "Moose" Ditty, the trainer for the Eagles, has worked out this progam that I've found helpful.

First Week

Jog one mile each day—
preferably across country with hills
Run stadium steps daily

Second Week

(Walk between drills)
1—440, ½ speed
2—880, jog
4—220, ¾ speed

Third Week

(Walk between drills)
1—440, full speed
1—880, jog
1—880, half speed

Fourth Week

(Walk between drills)
1—440, full speed
2—880, half speed
1—220, full speed

Fifth Week

(Walk between drills)
1—880 jog
3— 10 yd., full speed
4— 40 yd., full speed
3— 70 yd., full speed

Sixth Week

(Walk between drills)
1—880 ½ speed
1—440, full speed
5— 10 yd., full speed
8— 40 yd., full speed

Seventh Week
(Walk between drills)
1—440, full speed
3—220, ¾ speed
8— 10 yd., full speed
10—40 yd., full speed

Eighth Week
(Walk between drills)
1—440, ¾ speed
3—220, full speed
10—10 yd., full speed
10—40 yd., full speed

Generally speaking, those of you not coming out for a sport could cut this program about in half, and do it consistently for about a month. By then, along with your breathing exercises, you should be ready for some real body-building exercises. Getting in shape is one thing, putting on layers of muscles or stripping off that excess blubber is something else again.

12

How to Use Isometrics for Greater Health and Strength

The second phase of your body-building program consists of isometric contraction exercises and some other "motion" exercises. I am going straight to our training manual for this information. I am going to give you some of the very exercises with which the Cleveland Browns train. Trainer Leo Murphy has been with the Browns for a good many years, and has worked these out from his tremendous backlog of experience and knowledge. During the off season all of the Cleveland Browns players receive a manual from Leo through the mail, and we are urged to do these exercises. We believe we can increase our strength one hundred percent by a faithful performance of these exercises.

The principle of isometrics

Isometric contraction exercises are astoundingly simple, yet completely dependable. The only trouble with them is that it is hard to believe they could work. The principle is that strength and power may be built by bringing a group of muscles into a state of extreme tension and holding this tension for a few seconds, then relaxing. That's it, and that's all of it!

It is easy to overdo in isometrics, because it doesn't seem like you are doing much really. For that reason, isometric contraction should not be used to the point of fatigue. Actually, only about six exercises per workout are advisable and each of these is to be done *only one time.*

For this reason, isometric contraction should be used in conjunction with some forms of "motion" exercises to make a full workout. I am going to give you some of our isometric contraction cut down to about what I think you guys ought to be able to do; and then give you a series of motion exercises with which to finish your workouts.

You should work out twice a day, preferably before breakfast and just before your bedtime snack. By placing your exercise periods near to the time of eating, your body brings food nourishment straight to your muscles and really builds them.

Here's how you do it

The basic equipment for isometric contractions is a power rack. It is made by using a parallel bar with two standards (four-by-fours are best) fixed firmly to the floor and ceiling, having holes drilled to accommodate the placing of the parallel bar at different levels. This is a lot like a high-jump bar and standards, where the bar can be raised to any desired position, except that the bar should be inserted into holes that will hold fast. With such a bar as this, you will be able to achieve a number of stances and positions that will make it possible for you to exert maximum tension on many muscle groups.

Here are some exercises you can do that will build up certain muscles:

Shoulder shrug

Stand up straight against the bar which is adjusted at a height so that it will be in your hands when your arms are extended downward. Grip the bar with palms toward you. Now shrug your shoulders upward as hard as you possibly can. Don't bend either arms or legs. Put all the pressure you can on those shoulder muscles, breathe in deeply, holding the tension at the maximum count of six on the first trial. When you first grab the bar, begin to apply the pressure slowly, then increase to maximum strain and hold it at the maximum for at least six seconds. As you practice this, you can hold the tension a little longer; but you should not try to hold it more than ten seconds. If you do hold the tension beyond the count of six, exhale and inhale fresh air in the middle of your contraction—don't try to hold your breath more than about six seconds. This exercise will really build those shoulder and neck muscles.

Now here is the most important thing about isometrics. When you have done an exercise like described above, you don't need to repeat it during that workout. But you can work out twice or more a day. What you need to do is to develop about six or eight different contractions and go through the whole list only once and then stop. With isometrics you don't want to work to the point of fatigue.

So, let me give you about five more of these. A little later you may want to get a manual on isometrics and add a few more.

Military press

Set the bar about two inches above your head. Stand directly under the bar and grasp it with your hands about shoulder-width apart with palms outward. Remember, don't back off. Look straight ahead and push up on the bar as hard as possible with your leg, hip, and back muscles tightened like a spring. Get as much into it as possible and hold it six seconds—and longer as you practice—but remember to take a deep breath about every six seconds. Otherwise you might get dizzy. You must get the maximum strain—put as much power as you can into that contraction. Some guys fake it, but they're only cheating their own body. This one will really develop the arms, back, shoulder, and neck muscles.

Dead lift

Set the bar at a height where it will be about two inches below the knees. Grasp the bar with palms facing you about the width of your shoulders between your hands. Keep back and arms straight and bend the knees slightly. Now, push with the legs and pull up as hard as you can. Hold it six seconds or more. This will put the power in the arms, hands, and wrists, as well as the back and legs. This is also a pretty basic football position.

Rise on toes

Place the bar on the back of your neck, using a towel for padding, with feet flat on the floor about a foot apart. Be sure knees and body are erect and stiffened. Now, rise on your toes as hard as you can. Hold it four seconds or more. This puts power in the calves, and in the feet and ankles, as well as the neck.

Arm curl

Place the bar at a height slightly below the elbow joint when you are standing straight up between the standards. Grip the bar with the palms up and pull up hard on the bar. This one will really strengthen those biceps and forearms.

Bench press

Lying flat on your back, place the bar about twelve inches above your chest directly above the armpits. Reach up and grip the bar pushing straight upward for all you are worth. Hold a maximum strain for six seconds and release.

Finish your workout with these exercises

That is enough of the isometric contractions. These exercises will build power and strength into every part of your body. But, as I said before, isometrics contractions by themselves don't make a full workout.

I am giving you below some "motion" exercises to finish your workout. These exercises are designed to be repeated many times each workout; they don't require equipment. Try a few of these:

Wrist and forearm exercise

Double up one of your fists and place it in the palm of your other hand. Now swivel that fist in the socket of your palm resisting all you can by trying to keep it from turning with the other hand. Alternate and you will build a tremendous grip and strong wrists.

Push-ups

Oh yes, don't forget, probably the best exercise of all is the one you've been doing all your life. Plain old push-ups. Three sets of ten push-ups is a fine exercise to begin. Practice until you can do twenty without tiring. Try doing push-ups on your finger tips for a change. Always keep your body in a straight line while doing push-ups (keep your buttocks down).

Push-ups with applause

If you get to feeling real good, try this. At the topmost position of your upward push-up, quickly bring your hands together as if you were applauding yourself, and get your hands back in position to catch yourself before you fall flat on your face.

The rocking exercise

Lying flat on your stomach with your arms straight on the floor beside you, raise your head and your feet as if to touch the back of your head with your toes. You probably won't actually be able to do this; but you will have your body arched in such a way as to look like the rocker on a rocking chair. Now rock back and forth keeping the tension on your stomach muscles by trying to maintain the arched position.

Backward push-ups

Back up to a straight chair and place palms downward gripping the front corners of the chair. With heels out from you so that your back barely touches the front of the chair at the belt line, and keeping your legs straight, lower yourself until your buttocks are about an inch from the floor. Now, up again and repeat. Do several sets of ten if you can. Great for the triceps!

When this comes easy, get a friend to push down on your shoulders while you try to come up. Those triceps will really bulge out.

Sit-ups

One of the most important exercises on your schedule is the work on your abdominals. You can build these muscles by doing a number of sit-ups. Here's the way we do them in the pros. Lie flat on the floor with hands clasped behind your head. Bend your knees and put your feet flat on the floor, up as close to your buttocks as possible. Now bring yourself upright, keeping your feet flat on the floor and close to or touching your buttocks. You may not be able to do it at first, but keep at it until you can do at least three sets of ten repetitions.

Leg lifts

Lying flat on the floor with legs straight and heels on the floor at first, raise your heels up with legs still straight until your heels are about six inches off the floor. Hold this position about ten seconds. Now cross your legs several times while they are still suspended as if they were blades of scissors. Then without lowering the legs and never touching heels to the floor, lift your legs straight up without bending your knees, back over your head to touch the floor with your toes behind your head. Now bring your legs back again to the original position about six inches off the floor. Practice until you can do this ten times or more.

Chinning

The best exercise for building shoulders is plain old chinning. Practice until you can do twenty repetitions.

Hand stand and push-ups

If you really get good with all of these described already, you may want to try the hardest one of all. Do a handstand allowing your feet to go against the wall. Now while standing on your hands, do a series of push ups.

Don't try to do all of these exercises at one workout

Remember, I am giving you all of these exercises so you can have some variety. Don't try to do all of them at one workout. Do some running along with your isometric contractions, and choose some of these exercises to round out your program each time. And put some zip into it. Just keep thinking what a great set of muscles you are building.

13

How to Add Pounds and Build Muscles with Weights

Weightlifting is probably the most popular method of body building. The reason it's so popular is because you can *see* the results. In isometrics you can't see many results in muscle size, even though you do get stronger. You should start on the weights only after a thorough conditioning, strengthening, and toning operation. This should be done as I have suggested in the last two chapters. By all means be sure you are in shape before you go into the weightlifting phase. If you feel you must start right out on the weights, then start with very light weights and build up slowly.

Weightlifting is an every-other-day program

For best results, you shouldn't lift weights every day. A good workout on weights every other day is best, unless you want to work on different parts of the body on alternate days. You could do all stomach, leg, and back exercises one day and work other parts of the body the next day. But the point is that the same muscle shouldn't be worked two days in a row.

What's more, don't go into your weightlifting cold. Before you start on weights on any given day, you should run lightly through the "old stand bys" I gave you in the last chapter. Do a dozen or so push-ups, some sit-ups, and a stretching exercise for every major part of the body. You need to get good and warm before you touch the weights, so you won't pull a muscle. This would kill your progress.

The best way that I've found to do it is to work out on the weights one day and run the next day. It's best to lift weights just before the evening meal.

Start slowly

One of the real problems in weightlifting is that a young athlete fears getting hurt on the weights. This seldom happens, and only then when you get wild and sloppy. Other guys think it makes them slow. Nothing could be further from the truth. If you lift and run on alternate days, you can actually become faster.

There is little danger of getting hurt if you do these things:

(1) Warm up first. (2) Always work up a sweat before you start. You can do this by running in place, push-ups, and side-straddle hops. Hanging from an overhead bar will help you grow taller and stretch out your muscles while it gets you ready for the weights. (3) Keep your head up, your buttocks down, and your feet flat. When you pick up a weight, bend at the knees and waist.

Start very gradually at first, using light weights. But at the same time, you do need constantly to press your limits and gradually add more and more weight.

Now let's assume you have purchased a good barbell and dumbbell set. The set doesn't have to be expensive. You won't need an elaborate set, at least not at the beginning. With your set you will probably get a manual with a whole big series of exercises and instructions. The tendency is for you to go nuts doing the exercises just any old way and burn yourself out trying to do too much the first day. Actually, you would probably be better off with fewer exercises and a definite routine for doing them.

If you can do them in a group it's best for a lot of reasons. I've found that it's just like running, your time is never as good when you're running against a clock as it is when you're running against another guy. If you have to work alone you're always trying to do better than you did the workout before, but if you're competing against another lifter, you usually do better. Also, it's not as easy to skip a workout. Also, it's cheaper because rather than buying your own weights you can use the school's or the YMCA's. Many times a group will have an instructor; that is really the best.

Five good exercises for weights that will make those muscles bulge

I am going to give you five good exercises for weights that will make those muscles bulge, if you will just be faithful in doing them right. I should remind you here that the exercises can't build muscles, unless you furnish your body with the building materials in the form of food—but we are going to get to that in the next chapter. These five exercises will do the job for you, although you may want to change it up a little for the sake of variety, if you keep with it for several months. Actually, I think it's best to go on a three-months program and then take a little vacation, or at least change the exercises. You can get real stale on weightlifting after so long a time.

1. *The bench press.* This is one of the best. Get a strong bench like one that comes with a redwood picnic table. Lie flat on your back with maybe a towel under your neck and head for comfort. You must judge for yourself the weights you use according to age, size, and previous experiences with weights. The weights should be

light enough so that you can do eight repetitions, but heavy enough so that the eighth one will be tough to do.

To work out right with weights it's best to have a partner, sometimes called a spotter, working with you so you can help each other. Now, let your partner hand you the weight and let it down to the chest. Then press up, again and again. You might have better results if you bounce the bar off your chest. Learn to breathe in on the strain and out on the release, and always fill the lungs completely. Your lungs should be full when you are straining, because this builds your chest and enlarges your rib cage.

In weightlifting exercises we usually talk about sets and repetitions. The set is a group of repetitions numbering from two up. With your first efforts at bench pressing you should do no more than three sets of eight repetitions a day. After a week on the weights as described above, provided it is coming easy to you, add weight until you feel you are pressing your limit. Always add when the going gets easy, but never push yourself hard during the first week or two. The bench press builds arms, shoulders, and chest muscles.

2. *Curls.* Using a starting weight you can easily manage, stand erect, holding the barbell in front with palms upward. The barbell should begin at the thigh level. Now bend the body slightly forward and "curl" the barbell up to the chest, straightening your back as you come up. Lower barbell to the original position slowly, and repeat. This is tremendous for the biceps and should be done in three sets of six or eight repetitions. As you build your stamina, however, you will want to push your limit on weight. You'll really start seeing the difference in those arm muscles. It would be helpful if you could do your exercises in front of a mirror. You'll be able to see your muscles pump during just one workout. They'll go back down some, but not as small as they were. You can do this exercise more strictly by curling with your back against a wall. This way you don't cheat as much.

3. *French curls.* This exercise is done with one dumbbell which is held by the plates at one end. The exercise begins with the arms held straight overhead, then lowering the dumbbell to the back of the neck to complete a repetition. Doing three sets of six or eight

repetitions with weights that don't strain you is a good starting challenge.

4. *Military press.* In the military press, use a barbell you can handle easily. Bending at the knees and waist, you pick the bar up and pull to shoulder height. Never put the strain on your back. Put it on the legs by bending them every time you pick a weight up or put it down, no matter how light. Once you have it at shoulder height, you press it to arms' length upward, back down to the shoulders, then up again to repeat. Again three sets of six or eight repetitions is a good workout on this exercise. You should add weights as you find what you are doing is coming easy. Suck air in at the beginning of the upward motion, and continue inhaling until you have reached as far as you can upward. Exhale quickly on the downward motion.

5. *Bent rowing.* This exercise is done from a flat-footed position bending at the waist at a full 90 degree angle with your back straight, knees bent slightly. In other words, you are standing in a bent-over position. With a weight you can easily manage, reach down and grasp the barbell, pull the bar up to your chest and let it down until your arms are fully extended but without letting the weight touch the floor. Do three sets of six repetitions. Think of yourself rowing a boat, and you'll get the right idea. This one really puts power in the back and the lateral dorsae (muscles in your side covering the ribs).

Here's an example of what weights can do

In a Baylor University P.E. class, forty-eight male students were tested. Only three of the boys had more than forty inch chest measurements. After an eighteen week program of thirty-five minute workouts three times a week, only two had less than forty inch chests.

One boy picked up 6½ inches on his chest and the average was 3½ inches. The average on the arms in the same test was one inch.

On the shoulders the average was $2\frac{1}{2}$ inches, and the thighs averaged one inch bigger.

If this can be done in eighteen weeks with only three thirty-five minute workouts per week, you can see what could be done in a better program.

Here's the key to strength and gaining weight

There is one really basic thing to remember in weightlifting: If your main aim is to gain weight, you should do fewer repetitions with heavier weights. This pulls more nourishing blood into the tissues.

If what you want is endurance and loss of weight, you should do more repetitions with lighter weights. This toughens the muscle fibers but does not allow as much gain in weight or in muscle size. In other words, do three sets of twelve or three sets of twenty moderately heavy weights, but be sure you're tired on the last few repetitions. Chances are, most of you will be trying to gain weight, so you will be inclined to go to the heavier weights. Okay, but don't go at it too fast. Build up to it. Remember you can have fun with it, but don't show off and try too heavy a weight without proper build-up or warm-up. Another thing, in all the stooping exercises—let your legs do the work, not your back. You don't want a wrenched back. If you do come up with a muscle strain, you'll just have to lay off a few days until it heals. It is much better to take it easy and not lose the time a pulled muscle makes you lose. Remember there are three things to keep in mind when picking up or setting down a weight. Keep your head up, your tail down, and your feet flat.

I know that if you will stick to your weights faithfully you will gain your objectives of a glowingly healthy and beautiful body of which you will be proud. Stay with it!

I have one other word for you on this entire subject of body building. As important as your body is, it is not the most important thing there is. I have seen a lot of guys get on this muscle building kick and carry it too far. There is a certain amount of pride that is good, but it can be carried too far to the point of conceit. When this is done, you can become repulsive to your friends. Remember other people are seldom as impressed with your build as you are. For one thing, it makes them uncomfortable because it makes them ashamed of their own build.

If you are to be well-balanced, then you must be physically, mentally, and spiritually strong. An imbalance in any one direction is unfortunate. Thinking about your body all the time will cause you to be a hermit. You'll keep too much to your exercise routines, and away from people. I want you to be well-balanced—much of a man in your physical development, yes! But much of a man in your total personality.

I want you to put the things of God first in your life. Naturally, this means you've got to develop a good body, so you will have the strength to serve God—but, remember, your body is a means to the end of a dedicated life. You must as Paul says, "Present your bodies a living sacrifice unto God, which is your reasonable service."

14

Eat Your Way to a Powerful Body

It seems a little ridiculous that anyone should have to tell you how to eat. This is such a pleasant thing for most people that it does seem unnecessary. But what I am going to try to do is tell you how to manage your diet so that, along with your exercise program, you can either add pounds of muscle or strip off pounds of fat.

Most young men are underweight

While many of you are not underweight according to some doctor's charts, most of you do wish to add muscular pounds in the right places in order to round out your body. It's a real shame that so many of you guys just don't seem to know how to eat—or maybe you do know and just don't have the guts to follow the things you already know.

At any rate, I am going to give you some thoughts on how to eat so you can gain weight. There are three things involved here: First, you must eat enough; second, you must eat the right things; third, you must eat at the right time.

You should eat at least five times a day

The old idea of three meals a day is out while you're trying to gain weight. You've got to eat five! But get this—I do want you to eat regularly and not just accidentally. In fact, I don't want you to eat between meals at all—just five meals a day. To do this, obviously you must add two meals to your regular program. One extra meal should be eaten at about three-thirty in the afternoon, just after you get out of school, and another at bedtime (about ten at night). These two extra snacks should consist of some good energy foods including bread, a glass of milk, and dessert (ice cream, pie, or cake).

Eating is a habit, and you must get in the habit not only of eating, but of eating the right foods. If you habitually eat these five meals at a certain time, you will automatically get hungry at those times. So train yourself to the program of five meals a day.

Eating and your exercises must be timed right

For the best muscle-building results, your exercises should be done on a relatively empty stomach, and a meal should follow very soon after workout. It works like this: As you exercise, you draw blood to the areas of the muscles you exercise. This blood continues to flow for some time after you stop exercising. This blood should be rich with food nutrients. Therefore, your exercises should come just before you eat.

Let's say you work out twice a day. When you are on weights, you would do only one workout every other day but would supplement this with other workouts. At any rate, you should always do some brief exercises in the morning before breakfast. Your second daily workout might come at night just before your bedtime snack. When you are on weights you should grab a snack after school, wait about an hour and a half and then have your workout just before the evening meal, which most of you guys will have about five-thirty or six. This would be your second workout of the day. Be considerate of your mother and eat when the family eats regularly. Also plan your two extra meals so that you can fix them yourself.

Breakfast is important for a guy who wants to be healthy

I know a lot of you guys skip breakfast entirely, and others just grab a doughnut or something. This is bad and it's got to stop! Breakfast is your most important meal because at breakfast time it has been a long time since you have had anything to eat, usually at least eight or nine hours.

I know you'll say that you are just not hungry at breakfast time. Tough—you've got to learn to get hungry. In the first place, getting hungry is a habit. In the second place, if you get out of bed soon enough and do a fast five minute workout, you'll be hungry. I suggest that this brief workout be coupled with a quiet time of Bible or devotional book study and prayer. Review the suggestions I've given you in Chapter One concerning good devotional books.

The big trouble is that you don't get up in time to get the sleep out of your eyes and the early morning taste out of your mouth until you've gone to school; so you skip breakfast.

I want you to get up a full thirty minutes before your mother serves breakfast every morning. This will mean you'll have to go to bed a little earlier. First, drink some water or a big glass of fruit juice; then you are ready to get into those exercises. You'll be awake by the time you do a couple of dozen push-ups. Do the stomach exercises I gave you in Chapter Twelve and your stomach will be ready to get that food, digest it, and send energy racing to those muscles that are all warmed up and waiting to be fed. It may take you a few mornings to get used to this; but you'll soon find yourself liking it, especially when you see what it is doing for you. You'll go off to school whistling and happy with a full stomach rather than still half asleep. What's more important, you'll feel those muscles swelling, and you'll feel secure knowing that you've asked the Lord to lead the interference.

Here's what you eat for breakfast

Breakfast foods are the best of all. You ought to get some meat and eggs, some toast and cereal, some fruit juice, and above all plenty of milk. If coffee helps you get ready for the day, have a cup.

Let me give you a sample of one of my own breakfasts at training camp. First, I start off with a half grapefruit. Then I have some breakfast cereal with banana chopped up on it; then eggs, bacon, toast, and fruit juice. I want you to add a glass of milk. If you like coffee, have a cup, but don't skip the milk. Of course, if I'm overweight, I really cut this down a lot.

Be sure to get the essential foods, and plenty of them

Some people go toward the exotic foods for their diets, but that's not necessary for you. There's nothing wrong with yogurt, blackstrap molasses, and wheat germ, but you don't really need them. Chances are, your mother puts it on the table for you; but you will need to tell her what you want and like—usually, the common American foods do the job just fine.

I'm not going to prescribe what you eat meal by meal. Just be sure to get plenty of the following;

Milk—This has been called nature's most perfect food. Drink it—lots of it!I want you to drink a minimum of a quart a day, and remember, I said a minimum. That's only four glasses. You can have a soft drink at lunch time, but maybe you ought to drink the carbonated drink after you've had your milk. Try mixing some powdered milk with regular milk for more protein. A cup to two cups of powdered skimmed milk to a quart of milk really steps up the protein content.

There's nothing wrong with soft drinks, but don't make them a habit. I think this soft drink habit can hurt you. If every few minutes you drink a soft drink when you ought to be getting something with energy and protein like milk or hot chocolate, it's bad for you. I'm afraid that with all the soft drinks there isn't room in your stomach for the milk you must have.

Protein foods—Your muscles are mostly made of protein. So, if you don't give your body the muscle-building ingredients, how is it going to build them? You must eat lots of lean meat like steak, lean bacon, chops, roasts, and piles of tuna fish (if you don't have a skin problem). Avoid a lot of fat, and eat the lean red meat. Then you should have cereals, eggs, milk, and dried beans in abundance. All of these are protein-rich.

You should also take in as many grams of protein as the number of pounds you weigh in order to make you gain weight faster and to make you stronger. You can get protein in powdered form at the drug store, but the best and cheapest way is through powdered milk, as I suggested above. Protein is a *must* to rebuild the cells that are constantly being torn down by weight lifting.

Green and yellow vegetables—Many of you guys don't like vegetables. Trouble is you've never given yourself a chance to like them. I want you to broaden your taste and be prepared to try everything with an open mind.

Your body needs the roughage that comes from fresh salads made with lettuce, raw cabbage, and other greens. This is a source of the valuable vitamin C which keeps away the colds and puts zip into you. You need to learn to eat spinach and green beans, which give you valuable minerals in addition to vitamin C. You should also take about five hundred milligrams of vitamin C a day in tablet form. The yellow vegetables like squash and carrots give you vitamin A, and you get the starches you need from creamed corn and shelled beans and peas.

Potatoes—Potatoes are the great starch food. You need potatoes every day. It doesn't matter much in what form you eat them—creamed, baked, french fried, or in salad; but eat plenty of potatoes. And try sweet potatoes; they are especially rich in starch. If you are skinny, you need starches; if you are fat, you need to cut out starches.

Fresh fruit—Eat fresh fruit every day. The citrus fruits have vitamin C and all fruits are valuable in keeping you from having constipation. Apples and prunes are especially good for that. And bananas are great energy food.

Desserts—If you are trying to gain weight, you need plenty of desserts. Your mom has a tremendous variety, either homemade or available in the supermarket. Cakes and pies, ice cream, turnover pastries, doughnuts, and pralines. Boy, these are great and should really tempt your appetite; but if you are overweight, don't eat desserts.

Here are some special milk shakes that will put weight on you

I want to give you three special formulas for making milk shakes that will really help you gain weight.

NUMBER ONE:

Two or three ripe bananas
Four raw eggs
One and one-half pints of sweet cream
One cup of powdered milk
One quart whole milk
One-half cup honey

Place in blender or mixer and mix thoroughly. Place in refrigerator and drink a glass after school and at bedtime.

NUMBER TWO:

Two raw eggs
Three dips of ice cream
One-half can of sweetened condensed milk
One banana
One-half cup powdered milk

Mix in mixer or blender adding milk to desired thickness. Place in refrigerator and use as above.

NUMBER THREE:

Three-fourths cup powdered milk
Two teaspoons of wheat germ oil
One teaspoon cocoa
Two teaspoons of malted milk
Two raw eggs
Five teaspoons of honey
One dip of ice cream

Mix in mixer or blender and add milk to desired consistency. Place in refrigerator and use as above.

Suppose you are already too fat

Some guys seem to be naturally fat; they need to slim down. Well, you are just going to have to be selective in your eating; but you don't need to go hungry. There are plenty of things you can eat and make your muscles bulge, while your waist shrinks.

First, let me tell you what to eat a lot of. Protein! You really need to double up on protein. Look back over the protein list and pick out the things you like. Milk has a lot of protein, and although it has some fat in it too, you shouldn't cut out milk. Use skimmed milk.

The things you will have to stop eating are potatoes and other starches, bread, and desserts. Of course, it depends on just how overweight you are, how much you cut back. But, it's always better to leave off all starches. Don't even nibble on the starches until your weight is where it ought to be. Even then, take it easy. Don't let your appetite be your master.

With your exercise program, you shouldn't have too much trouble. You should bear down on the abdominal exercises and burn off some of those accumulated calories. Double up on running, too.

Suppose you have skin problems

This is a tough one for some of you guys. Here you are with your skin all pimply and broken out and you are skinny, too. If you eat the sweets, starches, and fats, your acne flares up something awful, and if you don't eat them you can't gain weight.

There is no easy solution. This condition will clear up when you get a little older, if you'll handle it right. It is *better* to stay skinny than to let your acne run wild. Stop eating the sweets, fats, and starches. See a doctor and he will give you the diet he wants you to have.

I'll tell you this; exercise is your best friend—especially outdoor exercise. You need to get out in the sun, wash your face at least three times a day, eat protein-rich foods, and just wait out a few years until your hormones straighten out, and you'll be all right.

What about vitamins?

Everyone needs vitamins. Most of you guys will get the vitamins you need if you eat correctly, as I have outlined. But here is the thing about vitamins: if you get more than you need, your body will just discard them, and if you get less than you need, you won't feel as well or be as healthy.

So the smart thing is to take some vitamin supplement pills and be sure. Just one of these a day will often step up your appetite and give you the essential vitamins at the same time. Ask your doctor for advice concerning the kind he would recommend, get some of these, and take them regularly.

Most all of the pros take some kind of vitamins. I take several multivitamins, wheat germ pills, vitamin C, and anything else that I can get. You can't get too many. The only thing that should slow you down is the price; and, obviously, you could waste money on these supplements since your body will use only so much and no more. Be sensible, but don't get the idea that only sissies take pills. If *that* is true, we have an awful lot of sissies in the pros.

15

Health and Strength Require Good Habits of Living

Exercise and diet are certainly important to good health. However, there are other factors that are important too. Among these are good habits of living that work along with your exercise and diet program to complete your physical development.

Water is the great purifier

We are blessed in America with good clean water and plenty of it. It is a health-giver when used for bathing and for drinking.

Bathing is for cleanliness, which certainly contributes to your health in many ways and also to your social acceptance by others. Beyond that, your bathing habits can put zest into your life, if you'll go about it properly. When you were a little boy, you probably hated to take a bath, but now that you are becoming a man, you must come to appreciate what proper bathing habits can do for your morale.

Start the day with a brisk shower

You will remember that I suggested that you give yourself plenty of time in the morning for your devotional time, exercises, breakfast, and grooming. In order to get to school with a zip in your step, you should take a good brisk shower after breakfast.

Start with the water lukewarm, lather up, and then rinse off with cool water—in the summertime at least, as cold as it comes from the tap. Step out of the shower and rub down with a coarse towel until you have a good pink glow all over. Then after you use a good deodorant, shave, and brush your teeth, you'll leave the house whistling.

Bathe again before retiring

Your morning bath is mostly for toning up, although you may be a little sweaty after a fast morning workout. Your evening shower is more for cleanliness and to prepare you to rest better. If you are on a weightlifting program or out for a sport, you will probably find it best to take your second shower right after workout and before your evening meal.

When I get sore from weightlifting or football, I like to soak in a tub of very hot water or get in the whirlpool at the field house. This is very relaxing after a hard day. If you stay in too long you'll get weak. We have a sauna bath in our field house which is also very fine for soreness. Steam is good, too. Of course, nothing that makes you sweat profusely, as all of these do, is good within two or three days of game time.

Drink lots of water

Drink plenty of water! This is something of a habit. You should be sure to have a glass before breakfast along with fruit juice; and you should stop at the fountain several times during the day. At training camp, they keep the fountains running all the time by taping the knobs to the "on" position to encourage us to drink more water. Why not make it a habit to never pass a water fountain without taking a drink? Drink some water immediately after workouts, but not too near to meal time. You will want all that space in your stomach for milk and food at mealtime. After a really hard workout, don't tank up on too much water. It can make you sick and will take away your appetite for sure.

During warm weather, especially if you are perspiring a lot, you should take salt tablets every day. Of course, if you have a skin problem, you should always use salt not iodized. If your body doesn't need the salt, it will throw it off. You can buy these at the drug store, they're cheap; they really help you to feel better and to avoid muscle cramps. Ask your coach how many to take. We usually take about four per meal.

Eat right to avoid constipation

If you want to be healthy and develop a strong body, you must have good elimination. Most of you know you've got to eat plenty of salads, vegetables, and fruit juices, or you'll be constipated. But what you don't know is that it also helps to develop a habit concerning when you should take care of "nature's call." Blanton Collier has reminded the ball club more than once to allow time for this after breakfast and before our morning workout at training camp. Most people find that just after breakfast is the best time to train themselves for this important habit.

The main thing is to have time for an unhurried elimination. If you have to hurry to make the car pool, you are not likely to eliminate completely; and there will be a build up in your bowels that will cause you troubles. Eat right, and make proper elimination a habit. This is a must for health and strength.

Sleep is the great restorer

You can't have a healthy body if you don't get the proper amount of sleep. It is true that different people require different amounts of sleep. The old idea of eight hours being the amount everybody needs is foolish.

Chances are at your age that you will need at least those eight hours, maybe more. You've got a busy life, no doubt about that; and maybe you don't figure you can spend a third of it in the sack and get everything accomplished. It is more than likely true that you sure enough can't get it all done if you don't get those hours in the sack. If you're lifting weights or working out for a sport, this is even more a must. In fact, if you don't get the proper sleep, it would be better not to work out.

Your level of alertness all through the day depends on the sleep you get. There is every reason to believe that you would be better off if you could have a nap after lunch—everyone seems to agree on that. But, let's face it; your schedule just won't allow it. Therefore, you must get your full requirement of sleep at night. Otherwise you'll be napping in class when you're supposed to be wide awake.

What is your bedtime?

Too many of you guys go to bed either when you are flat exhausted or when you get around to it. I want you to establish a regular bedtime and hit the sack right on time every night, or at least five nights a week. If you do that, your body will become accustomed to this timing and you'll go to sleep almost before you hit the bed. If you get your body all confused about when it is supposed to go to sleep, you may lie awake; or worse, you just won't get enough sleep because you go to bed too late.

That's the reason some of you drag around in the mornings—you don't go to bed early enough to get your rest. It's hard to say when you should go to bed; it all depends on when you must get up. But if you have to be at school by 8:30 a.m., you should be in bed at 10 p.m. You could get up at 7:00, allowing nine hours sleep, and have an hour for devotional time, exercises, breakfast, shower and shave. That would work out fine. If you can sleep a little longer on Saturday and Sunday, then you might stay out a little later the nights before—it's good to have an occasional break from routine.

If you feel you don't need nine hours sleep, you could make 11:00 p.m. your bedtime. If you have troubles getting up mornings, that should be a pretty good sign you aren't getting enough sleep.

Recreation is health-giving

In order to stay healthy, you need recreation. You've got to have some fun in your life. Tensions build up even in living normally; and recreation can help you to throw off the bad effects. If you get all wound-up, one way to unwind is to get into some vigorous recreation.

You should have something you like to do just because you like it. It may be a sport, but you should participate in this sport for the fun, not for exercise or for the competition. Some guys go out for football not because they really like it, but because they feel they must prove they are men or to be accepted by the girls. Maybe you like golf. Your father may play golf for exercise, but you should play for fun. Most things you do in life may be because you ought to, not necessarily because it's fun. So, you ought to do a few things just for fun.

The competitive sports aren't really very good for recreation, because you are likely to put too much emphasis on winning. Sure, you should play competitive sports, but what I'm talking about now is giving your body a chance to relax.

Active sports like tennis and golf do provide a method of releasing tensions. When you hit that little white ball a couple of hundred yards down the fairway, the tensions go with the ball. This is a psychological principle that works. You can just place your hostilities on the ball and knock the cover off. It's a healthy thing to do. Naturally, you aren't aware of doing this; if you thought about it all the time it wouldn't work. You don't have to visualize that ball as being your English teacher who really bugs you.

You should seek some recreational outlets both with people and by yourself. Occasionally, it does all of us good to have an hour or so all by ourselves to do something that interests us. Maybe you like reading, or woodworking, fishing, or painting. Give yourself the benefit of this relaxation.

Sharing fun is good for you

In search of relaxing good times, you will find that it helps to have someone to share these times with you. You can spend time with other guys, as well as with girls. You should have a girl friend by now who is really fun to be with, who likes some of the things you like. You can go bowling, play golf, tennis, picnic, ride horseback, and many other different and exciting things that girls enjoy. It's a lot of fun to teach a girl a sport such as this, and they're usually anxious to learn.

There are plenty of things that are relaxing to do around any town; things that in no way violate anyone's rights. Get the guys together and go fishing, coon hunting, skeet shooting—anything that you like and that's not destructive. Of course, there are other things to do that are upsetting to your parents, and that put you in a bad light. Night clubs, taverns and wild places are not for you.

To make your body healthy, control your mind

Your mind and your body are inseparable. Whatever happens to one affects the other. Many research studies in psychology show this to be true.

One psychologist was working with a man who had a hole in his abdomen so that one could see the tissues of his stomach through a very thin covering membrane. When he allowed himself to be made angry those tissues got all red and irritated.

That's the way your emotions affect your physical body. If you stay angry, frustrated, or tense, all the time, you could wind up with an ulcer. Anger and hate cause your body to secrete acids and other chemicals that will give you indigestion, headaches, and other difficulties. Try to live a calm, relaxed life, facing troubles and solving them.

A bad temper is a habit you don't want to get; neither do you want to go around all tied up in knots inside because you are filled with hate for some thing or some person. If you have a good disposition, you are much more likely to be healthy.

Many doctors estimate that as many as seventy-five percent of their patients are sick, or at least sicker than need be, because of emotional problems. A whole new field of psychosomatic medicine has developed to treat disorders of the body that are brought on by the emotions.

Don't go around sick

One of the worst possible health habits you could have is going around half-sick and doing nothing about it. Your body is powerful and strong enough to withstand disease, but there are plenty of bugs around that your body can't control by itself, no matter how healthy you may be.

You should have regular check-ups; and then when you feel yourself getting sick, see your doctor and get some medicine before this germ gets the jump on you. Fever is one of the main danger signs; but there are many others like sore throat, pain in chest or stomach, etc. Get some medical help, and stop feeling half-alive. I want you to be one hundred percent alive every day of your life!

16

Don't Be a Sucker About Smoking

It's really tough to have a rule against smoking in the pros. These players are grown men, most are married and have children. Now for a coach to come along and say his players can't smoke would be foolish.

But there are some coaches in the NFL who agree with Blanton Collier who said to us one day, "You men have a tremendous responsibility to the young people of America who look up to you. I think the least you could do is to refrain from smoking in public."

There are a few players on our team who smoke. They know it's not good for them, and some have quit. I think most of them wish they'd never started. The smokers on our team are in the minority. I know most of the players in the NFL, and I would guess the same is true in all of pro football.

There are some very good players who smoke; but I'm sure they'd be even better players if they didn't. At least they'd feel better which should affect their play.

Smoking or not smoking won't make you a Christian

When your pastor stands in the pulpit and talks about "sin," it is a fair bet that the majority of the congregation gets the idea that he's talking about three things: smoking, drinking, and sexual immorality. You ought to know that this is a fouled-up idea of the meaning of *sin*. Some people are big "sinners" who neither drink, smoke, nor participate in immoral sex. The best moral man in your church may treat his hired help like slaves, thereby stripping them of their dignity as human beings, or he may be cruel to his wife and children.

Don't get the idea that I'm saying you should quit smoking because it's not the Christian thing to do; I'm not appealing to you primarily on either a moral or a Christian basis. I just want to talk common sense. If you don't smoke, don't think you're a better Christian because of it. And if you quit, don't do it in order to be a better Christian. Your self-righteousness would be much worse than the habit. There are great Christians who smoke and many non-smokers who have no relationship to Christ.

We will consider the sex and alcohol questions in later chapters, but in this chapter I want to talk to you only about smoking. I realize there are many things worse, but we are trying to find the best way of life for you.

If you are going to stand tall and straight in the eyes of God, of your fellow man, and of yourself, you are going to have to make a decision concerning what you are going to do about smoking. There are two things that are bad about smoking. First, it hurts your health. Second, you should be the master of all your life. A man can't really stand tall if some habit has him cornered, and he has become an obedient servant to that habit.

Coaches know the facts about smoking

The last two coaches I've played for were non-smokers, and this is what they had to say about it. Paul Brown coached the Cleveland

Browns for seventeen years, and is probably one of the biggest names in the history of the pro game. He once said, "When I was a boy, I remember having a football hero. I thought he was the greatest. I went to see him play one day; and after the game, I went to the dressing room door hoping to see him when he came out. When he came out, he lit up a cigarette. I never will forget how disappointed this made me. I was determined that if I ever coached, I wouldn't let my players smoke, at least not publicly." Paul Brown lived up to that vow.

Blanton Collier, present coach of the Cleveland Browns, once said, "I used to be a smoker; but when my kids came along, I thought if my not smoking could keep even one of my children from getting the habit it would be well worth my stopping." He kicked the habit and hasn't smoked until this day.

Smoking has many people hooked

The worst thing that you could do would be to look upon those that smoke and feel superior to them. But in making your decision about smoking, it may help you to know that smoking can enslave you just as it has millions of other Americans. How many persons do you know who would give anything to be able to break this habit? There are only a few people who seem to be a little proud of the fact that they smoke. They often point out that for them it is a pleasure that they wouldn't give up for anything in the world. It is more likely the case that they can't give it up and that the claim that it is something they *wouldn't* give up is to save face for the fact that they can't.

Smoking is bad for your health

There is no moralizing involved in the statement that smoking is bad for your health. Common sense would tell you that it can't do your body any good to have these poisons drawn into the lungs and into the blood stream. But at this point in medical history, there is the irrefutable proof that cigarette smoking is a primary cause of lung and lip cancer, emphysema, high blood pressure, and heart disease. This isn't the statement of some straight-laced, kill-joy preacher—it is the medical statement of the surgeon general of the United States and is backed up by endless research, carefully documented. You and I know beyond a shadow of a doubt that smoking is a dangerous habit. Some say it is a good habit for them because it helps them release their nervous tension. This may make a little sense to those people who are already addicted; it makes no sense to you guys that haven't yet reached the point of addiction.

Most of you have taken a puff of the "weed" now and then. So what? You did this to show the guys you weren't a square. The trouble is, this habit sneaks up on you and you get that craving for the drug, nicotine. Then you're hooked and it takes real guts to break the hold it has on you. If you go too far with it, you just can't do it. Then you are a slave to this miserable habit for the rest of your life. When you think about the waste of money and health, the habit really stinks.

As a matter of fact, the habit is quite offensive to many people. Maybe you've heard the story of the guy who got on the plane and sat down by a man who was smoking. He pulled out a plug of tobacco, bit off a chunk and said to his neighbor, "You smoke and I chew. Tell you what, you don't blow your smoke on me and I won't spit on you."

There are still a lot of people around that have the feeling that smoking is the thing a real man does. If you don't smoke, you are just not one of the accepted crowd; you are a "chicken" and a weakling. Is that the way it is in your school?

Let me make a prediction. If you give in and do what everybody else does, ten years from now you will find that you couldn't care less what a bunch of kids think, but you'll still be hooked on the cigarette habit. And I'll make another prediction: ten years from now, the kids in junior and senior high school will have reversed themselves about smoking. It will go something like this, "Nobody but a fool would get hooked on the smoking habit." But you are of this generation, not of the next; so what do you do about it? You be smart about it—that's what. Don't be a fool and give up a healthy life for a little popularity that has to be gained by "pulling on the weed."

Even in this generation I am seeing the change, and you might just be lucky enough to find a group of sharp guys who already have gotten smart. Look around for a group of kids to run around with who are willing to face the truth and act on it. I'll bet there is a group like that at your school—a smart group that is secure enough about their manhood not to have to prove anything by this false standard of manliness. I really don't feel that there would be many groups that would exclude you because you don't smoke.

You are the intended victim of the cigarette manufacturers

If you knew personally one of the big stockholders in one of the big tobacco companies, chances are you would find him to be a pretty nice fellow. He would refuse to think of himself as a person who, for money, is willing to maim the young people of our land, to make them victims of a poisonous habit. If you asked him about it, he would probably say that he isn't at all sure that the reports on the harmful effects of tobacco are correct; that the new filters will make smoking safe; or that somebody is going to make them and that it is the using of them that causes the damage, if any, not the making.

This is perfectly logical so far as a given man is concerned, although some such persons may be having quite a fight with their consciences because they likely know the truth. But their living depends on tobacco products, and you can't really blame them for defending their way of making a living.

But let's look at it from the other side. The tobacco companies are in business to stay, at least they hope so; and they must have consumers for their products. The individual stockholder may be a pretty nice guy. But the things the tobacco industry is doing to lure young people like you into the habit of smoking are things I want you to be aware of.

Don't be a sucker

I'm not concerned so much with the survival of the tobacco industry. There are enough people already hooked on the habit to keep them rich. The one I'm concerned about is *you*. Few if any of you are really hooked. You are too smart to be a sucker, so that they can stay on top.

Who knows what will eventually happen? It may be that the government will close down tobacco manufacturing. Or maybe they'll perfect one of the tobacco substitutes. It's always possible that they really will find a filtering device to make smoking safe, or at least safer. The point is they haven't done it yet and may not in your lifetime.

So why be a slave to a habit? It takes guts to say "no" when the crowd says "yes." But you're a man with a mind of your own. I can't believe you are going to be so foolish as to fall for the smoking habit, and if you are already halfway addicted, why don't you back up and quit while you can?

PART FOUR

You and The People Around You

17

Help People Know and Like You

What you DO determines what people think about you

Just thinking back over the players I've known, the ones whom I've liked best have been the ones who freely compliment others. We usually play on Sunday, and on Tuesday we see the films of the game. And it's really interesting to see who gets most of the praise from teammates and coaches. It's usually the players who are best-liked. The good plays of the less popular players are overlooked or commented on less enthusiastically. But the good plays of the well-liked players bring a lot of praise. I've also noticed that the guy who praises the plays of others the most is usually praised the most himself. Of course, there are some notable exceptions.

To have a friend you have to be a friend

So far as you are concerned, people are important—they can make or break you. You must carefully consider means by which you may develop a winning way with the people around you. To be a success in this life, you must make people like you.

But, on the other hand, you cannot force people to like you. They will like you for what you are, and they will like you only if you like them.

For success and abundant living, you need people. A recent popular song declares, "People who need people are the luckiest people in the world." There is much truth in the words of the song, but it probably is more accurate to say, "People who know that they need people and who work to make the most of their friendships are the luckiest people in the world—and the most successful."

There are those who couldn't care less about people. They want to get as far away from them as they can. You have heard of the famous writer-philosopher, Henry David Thoreau, who became a hermit so that he could study the meaning of life through communion with nature at Walden Pond. Well, it would be hard to say just how abundant Thoreau's life was—anyway, that was a long time ago. A more modern writer has hit the nail on the head with the phrase, "No man is an island."

It's possible for a person to find a job where he doesn't have to mix with others very much, but in the long run he's going to have to deal with people in one way or another. So, even if you would like a career in bookkeeping or forestry, remember, the more people you know and the more friends you make, the happier your life will be.

As a Christian, you cannot dislike people, because your mission in life is to make others aware of God's goodness and grace. They are His people; and although you may find many things about them that seem to be out of order, remember that they, like you, are made in the image of God. Though the image of God within them is distorted by sin, it isn't completely destroyed. I feel that there is some good in every individual because there is something of God in every one of them. Even though they may reject his Son, God still loves them. They still have worth simply because they are made in His image.

How to USE people successfully—DON'T

It would be wrong for you to use people selfishly just to make you happy, although as I've said you can't be happy and successful without them. Working co-operatively with others will make for you a greater chance for success and satisfaction; and you can at the same time help other people have a happier, fuller life.

No matter what job you have to do it is seldom that you can do it well alone. Even in your future vocation as an adult, you'll need the cooperation of others. Remember, people want to be noticed more than anything else. They want to be made to feel important. If you'll be interested enough to show genuine concern, they'll follow you or help you in any way they can. It's very easy, and it doesn't take a second to comment sincerely on something you like about another person.

Compliment sincerely

Why don't you try looking for good things in others. And when you find them, then don't be timid about telling them if you genuinely feel it. Why don't you try saying things like this: to your mom, "Boy, that was a good meal." To a girl friend, "Your hair really looks neat fixed that way." To your teacher, "I really like the way you're handling this subject." Just make sure whatever you say is really true.

It's important for people to like you. They must see you as more than just another face in the crowd. But you must deserve this special attention by being an outstanding person. No matter how outstanding you are, if you don't really care about others, you'll miss a lot.

You may be thinking. "Are you saying that I should be a politician?" Nó! I'm saying you should really get down to what life is all about—loving others as you love yourself. And if you do love people, your concern for them can be strengthened by getting to know them better.

You are important

One of the greatest tragedies is that many people walk around with their heads down as if to apologize for living. They seem to think that nobody likes them. In fact, they think that everybody is either against them or doesn't care. The Bible says, "Ye are the salt of the earth, but if the salt hath lost its savour it is good for nothing but to be trodden under foot." This is a perfect picture of many people. They are very valuable, but they have lost direction and have become confused; so they have lost the feeling of being worthwhile. The saltiness is gone, they are weakened, and they've become valueless in making their world a better place in which to live.

Check your level of concern

A good way to check your concern for others is to listen to your next conversation with a friend and see if you're more interested in what he has to say or in what you are planning to say when he quits talking. Could it be that you're just waiting until he gets through talking so that you can tell him about yourself or what you're interested in? If this is so, you're not really interested in *him* at all. You must develop a concern about your friends. Get to know their backgrounds. Ask questions that will help you get to know them better.

People WILL like you

You must feel that people will like you and that you can like people. You could say to yourself and to the person you hope will be your friend something like this: "Here I am, a person of great worth. I want to know you, because I know you are a person of great worth, too. I know that I would like you if I really knew you. And I know that you will like me. And if I got to know you real well, I'd like you even better." Of course, you say all this with your attitude and actions. It would probably sound silly if you said it aloud. But you should sincerely feel this.

With this attitude you'll meet others with your head held high. You won't be expecting the impossible from people, because you know they make mistakes just like you do. Being human is the most wonderful recommendation you could have. Never forget that God thought that humans were so important that he sent His Son to die, so that they could have life.

With this attitude you'll meet others with your head held high. You won't be expecting the impossible from people, because you know they make mistakes just like you do. Being human is the most wonderful recommendation you could have. Never forget that God thought that humans were so important that he sent His Son to die, so that they could have life .

Yes, you need people, and people need you. You will be almost a sure shot for success if you really like people. With such an attitude you will be well-equipped to be of maximum service to God and His purposes in the universe.

18

Parents Are Important People

The two most important people in your universe

Parents are a lot like coaches. Some parents and some coaches are tough-minded. They think they are the big authorities on everything. And to tell the truth, they are people of experience and wisdom, at least as a rule.

Some parents start out tough, and some of them stay tough. Some coaches do the same. On the other hand, some coaches are smart enough to realize they can't be successful without every player on the team playing his best. The way to build this success is through building a winning attitude into his players. So he treats them with respect in order to make them confident. Some parents also realize their success depends on the confidence they instill into you.

You can't expect parents to have confidence where no confidence is due, but parents should be aware that confidence must be kindled and built much like a campfire. It starts slowly in you, and they build it into a roaring flame.

Take the National Football League. When I first signed with the Cleveland Browns, we had a coach that called all the plays from the sidelines. We had a good quarterback, but the coach didn't seem to have enough confidence in him.

No quarterback wants every play called from the bench. On the other hand, any smart quarterback realizes that in certain critical situations, the coach on the sidelines, who is in constant communication with his assistants watching from a point high up in the press box, can give him some pointers and even some plays that mean the difference between winning and losing.

Watch the quarterbacks in the NFL today. They call most of the plays. But when the going gets tough you'll see Frank Ryan trot over during a timeout to have a word with Blanton Collier, or Don Meredith trot over to Tom Landry.

They know they've got to help each other. They don't sweat it. The quarterback is king of the gridiron, but he takes advice when he needs it. The coach sends in a play when he thinks it'll help. The quarterback must be teachable enough to listen to the coach and his assistants, who are looking at the game not only from a better advantage point in the press box, but also from the point of view of many years of experience. When you combine the quarterback's confidence he develops right there on the field of combat with the experience of the coaching staff, you have a winning combination. That's the way it ought to be between you and your parents.

Your parents are the two most important people in the universe so far as you are concerned, whether you like it or not. The Freudian psychologists insist that most of the good qualities (as well as the unwanted behavior patterns) you now have are the result of relationships with your parents during your early life.

This makes sense; your parents have contributed nearly everything to the pattern of what you are and what you will become both in the sense of giving you a heredity, and building within you habits, ideals, and dispositions both good and bad. You can thank them for the good; and since everybody makes mistakes, you can't be too tough on them for the errors they have made. They probably thought they were doing the best thing for you at the time. Your parents' biggest problem is like the biggest problem of the coaching staff—to know when to call a play for you, and when to let you figure it out for yourself. Lots of times when the coach calls a play from the sidelines, everybody wishes he had let the quarterback call it. Coaches make mistakes and parents make mistakes; so try to be understanding. You have to admit that there are times when you make mistakes, and you may really welcome some coaching from your parents.

You may resent your parents

It is really easy for you to resent your parents. The cards are sort of stacked in that direction. You want to grow up, and you think your parents don't want you to. You see their discipline and continual preaching in one direction or another as stunting your growth. Or it could be that they really in fact don't want you to grow up. Also, there is a natural conflict between the old and the new. It's sometimes a conflict between the younger generation struggling for new and better things and the older holding onto an antiquated past.

Of course, parents of one generation can't always see eye-to-eye with young people of a new generation; but there is really no need for the problem to get so big that it creates a break in the relationship that means so much to you and your parents. Parents shouldn't allow these breaks in communication to occur, but there are times when it is impossible to keep relations friendly and smooth. But you must also realize that it is your responsibility to try to solve the differences and at least meet your parents halfway. When you were a child, it was mostly up to them to work out your problems. Now that you are becoming a man, you must realize that you've got to take your share of the blame if you don't get along. Sometimes the temptation to stay mad at your parents seems too big to forget. But be as big about it as you can.

Getting along with parents

You must try hard to keep the warm relationships you now have with your parents or to restore that which you have lost. Try to get them to meet you at least halfway. If you foul up here, life can be a real drag.

The Bible says, "Honor your father and your mother, that your days may be long upon the earth." This is true, but it could go farther and say that your days will also be a lot happier. There is no conceivable way that you can be at odds with your parents and be happy and productive down through the years. This kind of resentment can really get to you. Remember, you respond to people around you with whatever feelings you have for your parents. For instance, you can't expect to be on good terms with your teachers, if you aren't on good terms with your parents.

It's probable that you think your mom and dad are people who tell you what you can or can't do. They seem to hold your whole world in their hands.

There is no denying that some parents think of themselves as firm dictators and decision-makers for their children. If they're that way, they unnecessarily upset you with their heavy-handed tactics. But just about every parent has the same goal, which is helping you to grow up to be a mature, well-rounded, and self-supporting young adult. They don't all go about it in the same way, but who is to say what is the "right" way to deal with young people? I find that it's a much harder job to be a parent since I've become one. I was certain before I became a parent I was going to be the best possible. But since I've been one, I've discovered it's not quite so easy after all. In fact, I constantly find myself resorting to the easy way out. I find myself sometimes getting the problem solved in the quickest possible way and getting it over with, even if it means being a bit harsh and unreasonable. I guess all parents are like that.

Look ahead to your days of parenthood

It's a little hard for you to believe it right now, but in a few more years you are going to be a mature, self-sufficient adult, with high earning power and full control of your life. Don't you hope that your parents will be able to produce, in you, a fully responsible person who looks life straight in the eye and who knows just what to do and how to do it? If their methods will accomplish this for you, more power to them!

Life is short. It won't be too long until your parents will be getting old. Then it will be you who will be "calling the shots" for them. You will be deciding for and with them whether it is best that they sell certain properties, take on certain responsibilities, etc. They won't always be the power figures; and neither will you, because a little further down the road it will be your children who will be looking out for you rather than taking orders from you.

When you take a look, surely you will be able to take in stride what may otherwise seem to be unreasonable "meddling" in your private affairs by your parents. They aren't "meddling" really—they only want the best for you. Even though parents are often wrong, you should be willing to believe that their mature judgment about many things is better than yours. And you may be sure that the values and ideals which your parents think are important, aren't really so drastically old-fashioned and out of date. You will probably impose the same values on your own children that your parents are creating in you.

Parents aren't perfect; you must love them in spite of their shortcomings

But let's be honest about it. Some parents are uninformed about some things and are completely confused about others. And some parents let their own personality problems color their thinking and discipline of their children. And by anybody's standard, they are sometimes mean and hateful.

It's tougher for you if you have parents like that. However, you still owe them the "honor" that the Bible speaks about. Your anger at their injustices blinds you to the valuable things they are passing on to you. It could be that they are doing a great deal to turn your life toward the finer things. At least be fair in your judgment of them and their ideas.

But, even if your honest appraisal leaves them far behind in being really "good" parents, you should remember that there are a lot of things about your parents' background that you don't really know. If your parents have traits which are antagonizing, try to understand that they, like you, are acting that way because they are yielding to the influences of their own past experiences. They may have had many unfortunate experiences that you don't know about. You must learn from their mistakes, so that you won't make the same blunders.

Love your parents *because* of what they are, and if you have to, in *spite* of what they are.

19

Teachers Are Special People

A few years ago, one of the teams in the League got a couple of their running backs hurt right in the middle of the season. The ball club was considering hiring a friend of mine to play for them for the last half of the season. He had all the physical equipment. He was big, strong, and fast. The coach said, "I think we'll take him on at a good salary, but first we've got to check with his college coach." As it turned out my friend didn't get the job. He and his college coach never got along. When the coaches called, he said, "No, you don't want him; he's a trouble-maker." My friend was terribly disappointed because he had his heart set on getting to play in the National Football League. He thought the college coach was terribly unjust for "bad-mouthing" him, but that's the way the ball bounces. And it shows how important it is to try to get along with others.

You should be fully aware that the people who can be of maximum help to you in achieving your goals are those older than you. It's a real compliment to a young person to be friends with people of all ages, and it's usually easier than you think. To be liked only by people your own age is not much of a compliment; rather it suggests that you're sore at the largest part of the world, that is, people older than you. You need the friendship of those your own age, but you need the friendship of your elders even more.

Teachers help shape your pattern of thinking

It isn't always easy to be on good terms with people older than you. There are times when it seems as though you must show hostility toward them in order to stay with the "in group." I've seen guys act smart to an adult in order to "show off" for friends. This is something you will have to fight against constantly. But don't forget, by acting this way—you are thinking only of the present. You must also think of your future. It is important that you have a good time now, but also it's important for you to remember the future. In a few short years you're going to want a certain job real bad. Your possible employer will check your records in high school and college carefully. If they are good, you've got the job. If not—you guessed it; you get the cold shoulder.

Teachers are among the most important people you will ever know. There are many reasons why this is true. Of course, your teachers are important because of what you will learn from them—the subject matter they will put into that brain of yours. There is real truth in the old saying, "You are what you think."

Your teachers mold your personality

But even more important than the actual knowledge you get, your teachers have a tremendous influence on your personality. Most of them are anxious to influence you in the best way. Most of the teachers you'll have are people of fine character and high ideals. They are likely to be dedicated people with deep interests in developing your mind toward its highest potential. Most of your teachers are making a financial sacrifice in order to teach you. They could make more money doing almost anything. Maybe some day you'll be on a school board and in a position to raise their salaries; but in the meantime, the best thing you can do is to be appreciative.

Now, of course, it is true that there are some teachers who are using the profession as a stepping stone to something bigger for them; and there are undoubtedly a few who are teaching because they can't get a job doing anything else. But even these have something of wisdom to offer. If you'll let them, all your teachers will help you. I challenge you to try to get along with every teacher you have. Even the real gripey ones can be reached, if you'll really try. In fact, they may be the easiest ones to be friends with, because they usually need a friend more than anyone.

Your success in school depends largely on your personality

One thing is sure, if your teachers like you and you like them, you are a lot more likely to succeed. You may have thought that because a teacher had it in for you, she gave you bad grades. You may just be imagining it. But let's face it—teachers are people, and they are sure to respond to you on the basis of their liking for you even when they are trying not to be prejudiced, etc.

The smart thing for you to do is to see to it that your teachers like you. But how can you do that? Simple! There are certain things that are disturbing to any teacher. Remember, everybody has a pet peeve. You are smart enough to figure out any point of friction, but here are a few reminders:

Study your teachers and try to please them

First, you should be aware that teachers face a tough job in dealing with a room full of students who don't always act their age. If you talk excessively, don't pay attention, create distractions, and things like that, you can hardly expect to have the teacher like you.

Secondly, it is only natural that teachers feel that their subject is very important. Maybe you don't feel the same way about it; but if you are to be a winner with the teacher, you must show as much interest as you possibly can to make the teacher feel appreciated, while winning a friend for yourself.

You certainly do not want to be superficial about this. But if you will honestly try, you can find interest in any subject. But even if you have to force yourself all the way, you are better off. It is almost certain that you'll really start liking it at least a little bit. By sitting on the front row, listening carefully, and taking part in the discussion, you'll probably develop a genuine interest.

Your school record is a permanent thing

You must know that the grades you make in school are put down in a permanent record and are passed on to your college, sometimes to employers, and even to your draft board. Don't let anybody kid you; grades are important. And you should always remember that the grade you make in English Literature is only partly determined by the amount of subject matter you have acquired. A large factor in your grade will inevitably consist of how your teacher evaluates you as a person. Fair or not, that's the way it is.

You must also remember your grades are only a part of what your teachers put on record about you. They are asked to rate you on many personality features such as dependability, willingness to work, cooperativeness, etc.; and these ratings go into your permanent records, too. You can't afford to have anything but the best of ratings.

Many times your teachers will be asked to fill out recommendations for you. This continues many years past the time of your graduation, so try to make your impression on your teachers a good one.

Teachers know apple polishers when they see them

Teachers usually know when you're apple polishing; but this isn't always a bad thing. Sure, you should avoid being an obvious phony in all things; you should try to be sincere and genuine all the time. But teachers will respond to your efforts to get them to like you in a positive way, provided it's not overdone. Even though they know that you are trying to impress them, they'll like it and will accept you, even if you aren't as subtle as you ought to be. Most of the time they will think well of you for having the good sense and energy to try.

Again, if you want your teacher to really like you, you must genuinely like the teacher. And there is every reason in the world why you should like them. Just think about their problems and you will be quick to overlook what may seem to be weaknesses. Chances are you wouldn't do half as well if you were in their place.

20

You Must Win The Confidence of Adults

You are fast becoming a young adult. Some adults may treat you like you are still a child. If you want to be treated like a man you must prove that you deserve that much respect. If an adult doesn't try to help you or even if your parents seem to want to treat you like a little boy, you should act mature. Don't stomp and snort like you did when you were a child. As the apostle Paul said to Timothy, "Let no man despise thy youth." This is the charge you must hear and heed. You are a man; and you must be determined to be recognized as such.

Some primitive tribes put their young men through various painful rituals that are called "rites of passage." One African tribe initiates their young men to full status of manhood by pressing a mat of hundreds of stinging wasps to their chests. If they show no signs of pain, they have won their places. This seems pretty drastic, and yet it may be easier for the African youth than it will be for you. At least he passes the test once and for all, and from then on he is given adult status without further question.

You must develop associations at the adult level

You are very lucky if your parents are completely willing to have you grow up and run your own life. But don't blame your parents if they hang onto you as though you were still a child. They just can't believe that you are growing up.

Your parents will usually give you freedom if you really act like a man. If you continue to act like a child, you can't really blame them for treating you like one. On the other hand, you shouldn't go directly against your parents' wishes. Also, you should move slowly into adulthood so that it may be an easier change for you as well as for them.

Now the time has come for you to be a man of your own. This doesn't mean that you won't need your parents' guidance; and it shouldn't mean that you get mad and hold a grudge against your parents when they try to help you.

Try it this way. Pick out some activity that your parents have usually babied you with, as if to hold your hand so you wouldn't fall or stumble. For instance, suppose it is time for your dental check-up. If your mother or father have always gone along, go without them. There is nothing worse than a young man who lets his parents practically run his life for him. Be kind and gracious with them, but be determined to do some things for yourself, too.

Just tell your parents what you have done as matter-of-factly as possible and watch their reactions. If they approve, then take some further steps toward independence. Don't go too far too fast, though; and if the thing you have in mind is too far out, then maybe you should clear it with one or both parents.

Let's face it. A man needs to be independent in matters involving his health habits; and you can be. You don't need someone to push you to see the doctor when you're sick, and you don't always have to have your mother along when you're buying clothes if you stay within the budget.

Be practical while developing independence

You probably depend on your parents for financial support, and you may have to depend on them for several more years. You can't really be self-supporting until you finish school, and if that means college, then you can't very well finish school and hope to be self-supporting at the same time.

Your parents love you and want to support you until you are able to support yourself, and that means they will have to help you financially for some time after you actually become a man. So what? That doesn't mean you are any less a man. You live in a culture which requires a lot of education, and your only other choice is to quit school. But if you quit school, you almost cut your throat in the race for success. We live in a highly competitive world that puts a premium on education.

High school is practically a must for everyone. College is important for most of you; and a graduate school education will be helpful to many of you. While college is not a must for all of you, you should get as much education as you possibly can.

So let your parents support you for the most part. If you can help out by earning your spending money and a little more, great! But don't sacrifice education for pride, whatever you do. And don't forget to be appreciative for the education that may set the "old man" back well over ten thousand bucks. It wouldn't hurt to say sincerely, "Thanks, Pop!"

The high school drop-out is going to be forced to take a lot of jobs and do a lot of things he really doesn't like. He'll probably be sorry he didn't keep going to school those extra few months or even years. Remember, your earning power will be increased by several hundred thousand dollars over your lifetime, in all probability.

Here are some of the areas for your independent action

As you start becoming a man, you should build a friendship with a number of specific professional people. Here are some of them: Every man needs a physician, a dentist, a banker, a pastor, and a lawyer. Of course, there are others, but these are the main ones.

Now the professional men you choose to help you into adult status may be the same ones your father uses. A lot of times this is a real advantage if your father has a good reputation. But it might also be good to choose one or two people not on your father's list. It's best that you both have the same pastor, because church relationship is a family thing at least as long as you live at home.

But you may choose a banker that your father doesn't use, or a barber, etc. There is certainly no reason for you to go against your father's advice in choosing these important people, and in some cases you may really need him as a reference. For instance, if you want to borrow money, the banker may require your father to co-sign the note with you. That's all right; it's your debt and you are going to pay the money back.

Your father is going to be proud of you as you grow up. He's going to want to help you in any way he can. He may feel that it's best for you to go it alone on many things; and, on the other hand, he may feel that you need some coaching on certain projects. Take his feelings into account. The chances are he is as anxious for you to get to manhood as you are yourself. Even if you think your dad is really "out of it" at times, show him respect; and remember, you owe him a lot.

Always treat the people you choose as your advisers (bankers, clothiers, etc.) with great respect, and yet show them that you have confidence in yourself. If they have shaky confidence in you at first, because of your youth, their reservations will disappear as soon as they find out you mean business about becoming a man. Remember the scripture that says "When you become a man, put away childish things."

Never be afraid to try some things on your own. Very few successful people were born rich, and many times those who were rich lost it one way or the other. When you start doing some things on your own, becoming independent of your parents, it won't take you long to realize that I was right when I said, "You really need people." Try it and see!

21

Women! Boy, Are They Important!

Suppose you were a young man in the days Christ walked the earth—nearly two thousand years ago. Suppose you had a date with a girl to go to the chariot races. Boy! It sure would be a lot different from now.

When Christ came he really made some changes

In those days, women were treated almost as slaves. They had little status. Usually, wives trotted along behind their husbands like obedient dogs. They had to cover themselves from head to toe with long robes and in some parts of the world had to wear veils when walking on the streets.

It would turn out to be the kind of date you guys would call "gruesome," because this girl likely would be closely chaperoned. It would be a real "drag." But the worst of it would be the personality of the girl. It is hard to imagine that she would be able to hold her head high, proud of being a woman. She wouldn't be much fun, you can be sure.

Christ changed all that. Because of His life and teachings, women today have found their place as equals to men. No longer are they seen as creatures to be used for the purposes of men. They are people of great worth principally because Christ elevated womanhood to its present importance.

Women make mistakes

All women aren't angels. They make mistakes just like men do. They have much the same temptations you do. It has been said that nothing is as bad as a bad woman; and this has been well illustrated by Jezebel in the Bible.

But your attitude toward women in general should be one of courteous concern, because women are special creatures, gifted with qualities of softness of manner and voice, gentle, and sweet. Sure, there are a lot of them that aren't that way. But at least give them a chance. If they prove to be anywhere near what a real woman should, then offer them the proper respect.

Obviously, gentleness and sweetness in women varies widely. Some are hard and almost masculine; others are overly fragile. Most are somewhere in between. But, your reaction to women isn't completely dependent on how the women themselves act. Many times your attitude toward them has more to do with your mother. Some of you have been very fortunate to have mothers who were warm and affectionate, kind and considerate, making your boyhood a time of joy. If you had a good mother who was warm toward you but not overly dominating, you will have set your mind on the goodness of women. But what if your mother was pressured by many problems and worries and was unable to give you a warm love and a happy home life? Should you then get mad at all women, taking every possible opportunity to get even, to show hostile reactions toward them?

You are only human, and, if in your judgment you didn't receive as a child the warmth and love that would help you to have an optimistic personality, it is likely that your reactions toward women are bad. You must take a look at your feelings toward women right now. If you are hostile toward the women in your life, *now* is the time to change.

You must understand that your mother, living under the pressures she faced, did the very best she could. You can't tell, maybe your dad was an alcoholic. Maybe she was jealous of him and had good reason. Maybe there was a money shortage that made her overly sensitive. Or she could have been in bad health. It is probable that she is even more aware of her failure than you. She wishes she might have been more warm and loving, and would give anything to be able to go back and live those crucial years over again.

Now you are old enough to understand and forget the past

But now that you are old enough to understand, you will realize the great love your mother has for you and you will show her in little ways and at various times your love and appreciation. If you have a warm relationship with your mother, you will probably have a warm relationship with all females for the rest of your life. If you are going to live a happy, exuberant life, you must have good relationships with a wife, who will share so much of your life.

One thing is certain—you can change. You can rise above whatever your background may be. If you are willing to admit your problem with women, you can lick it if you try hard enough. You are influenced by your background and your present environment, but you are still responsible and in control of your attitudes.

It's obvious, you can't live without women. Man and woman were made for each other, to complement each other physically, mentally, and spiritually. You will find that women fill an important place. It is unthinkable that you could live a balanced and adjusted life without warm relationships with members of the opposite sex. As mothers, they love you, discipline you, train you, and do a thousand other things for you. As girl friends, they give life happy dimensions socially. As wives, they share the joys of building a home and family. Think about it and you will know that this is true.

Women are able to make many things come your way

I've already emphasized that it's a mistake to try to figure every angle so that you can use other people to accomplish your own selfish goals. It seems a little selfish to suggest that you should purposefully learn and practice courtesy toward women so as to have them on your side—so that you can gain a personal advantage. If you practice courtesy or flattery toward women and get them on your side *just* to use them for your purposes, you are wrong—wrong even if they don't figure you out. Usually, however, you can help them to feel important while you make a friend at the same time—it's not all one-sided.

Women are powerful in our society

So face up to it: Women are powerful figures in this world in which you live, they control many things that you must have in order to achieve the full life you are seeking. Think of it: most of your teachers so far have been women, and many of those you will have in college will be. Everywhere you go, no matter what your goal, you are going to be faced with a woman who has something to say about whether or not you are allowed to succeed.

Cultivate a gracious attitude toward women

So, cultivate this gracious attitude. If you are a Christian, then you should realize that women are something very special to begin with. Learn and practice the very special things that please the typical woman. Be quick to offer your chair, to help her across the street, to open doors for her. Remember any woman deserves these courtesies. Treat every woman the way you would want every man to treat your mother or sister; and you will win friends, both male and female.

PART FIVE

You and Your Values

22

Values Are Private Affairs

You will develop some ways of thinking as a young adult that will stay with you for the rest of your life. There are some things you'll do socially, and some you will refuse to do. You need not feel that you've given up anything of real value. It is *not true* that you must take part in all the social activities if you are to become a real man. The opposite may be true; your participation in some questionable social affairs marks you as an immature person, a crowd-follower, and a gutless wonder. If your friends get the feeling that you really don't want to go somewhere or to do something but you do it just to please them, they won't really respect you.

You must be responsible for yourself, but not a moral policeman

Some may say, "Come on, be sociable, take a drink with us." But if they realize that you really don't want to and you let them push you into it, they're not impressed. Social maturity doesn't depend on following the crowd. You may feel a little uncomfortable at certain affairs if everybody is doing something you feel is wrong. But this doesn't mean that you can't be friends with everyone. You must not be a moral policeman trying to clean up the morals of friends. Even so, you should let your own values be seen, so as to swing your influence concerning what is right and wrong.

There are a lot of groups and social events you can be involved in and feel perfectly comfortable. All you need to do is choose those which are in agreement with your own feelings and get involved in these groups—but don't feel self-righteous about it. You know certain things are wrong for you; you can't always judge for the other guy. Some of those whom you would like to call personal friends will have different ideas of what makes a good time. Maybe you don't agree with them on some things, but you can find a lot of other things in common with them. It may stretch you a little, but you can be friends with everyone; and you'll be a bigger person by including everyone as your friend.

Your closest friends will be those with whom you have most in common. There are a lot of people who think as you do about things, and many others who think enough like you to still be fairly close to you. These two groups will form the two inner circles of friends. Then will come many other circles outside of that, until everyone fits somewhere into the orbits of your friendships.

Choose girls who are like you are

It doesn't take long to tell if a certain girl has the same set of values for her life that you do. If a girl smokes or drinks and you are convinced that these habits are not for you, then you'll probably be better off just passing her by, no matter how good looking she may be. I know this really may be hard for certain minority groups where there aren't too many girls to choose from. There may be few in your religious or ethnic group, but even if you belong to such a group, you should make this a matter of serious concern.

It's really a good idea to have a long talk with any girl about whom you seem to be getting serious. Find out how she feels about the important things; and if she's not in agreement with you, then you can let things cool off gradually, so as not to hurt anyone's feelings. You should allow her the right to feel the way she wishes about these key issues, but you shouldn't "chicken out" on your own convictions. If you do, it will always be a source of trouble in your relationship with people.

You are still in the process of building values

To a certain extent, you have adopted the values of those who are close to you, your parents, your pastor, etc. This is fine, just the way it should be. And there is no reason why you should undergo any drastic change in values as you grow older. On the other hand, you may find yourself modifying the values you learned as a child. That's all right, too.

Values are for the most part relative, not absolute. But it is healthy for you to have a somewhat stable value system that is able to guide and keep you moving toward a worthwhile goal all your life. Don't worry if you aren't quite sure of what you think about certain things. Just go slowly, consider every side of every question, and you will come out with a workable system. The Bible is the prime source of a good value system; but it must be properly interpreted.

A great many young people are rebelling against the value systems of their parents. There is no need for rebellion. You'll probably end up placing value on the same things they do; you'll wind up agreeing, to a surprising degree, with your parents' basic thinking in most areas. There's probably nothing wrong with the value systems of your parents—at least their value systems are not bad just because they are so sure they are right. Neither do you need to hold to the values of your parents just because they *are* your parents.

You do owe your parents something

On the other hand, any thinking young person will come to the conclusion that he must listen to and consider what his parents think is right or wrong in each situation. Just listening without blowing up may help a lot. Your parents are important people, they have given you a big start in life; and so long as you are under their roof, you ought to consider their feelings. Sometimes you will have to make decisions which will pit your parents' points of view against some things that you yourself have come up with. The question then becomes: "Should I strike a blow in favor of progress, or should I consider my parents' feelings?" This really is a hard problem; you really have to sweat out these situations. The trouble is that many times you aren't positive you're right.

For instance, suppose your parents have taught you that any kind of night club is a bad place. And perhaps you have come to feel that some of them aren't so bad, and you could have a good time there even at your age. Let's say that your parents aren't obnoxious about it; that is, they don't forbid you to go, but they certainly let you know they'd be better pleased if you didn't. Should you strike a blow for the liberal view and *against* what you consider straight-laced old fashion thinking, or should you give in and do what your parents want?

There's no way for me to say what you should do. I would urge you to consider every side of the question. In the first place, don't take for granted that your parents don't know what they're talking about—there's a good chance that they are basically right. I'll admit some of your parents are awfully narrow-minded and hard to reason with. But if you expect them to sit down and quietly discuss the situation with you and listen to your side, then you must be willing to listen to their side. Remember, they've been around longer than you have.

Don't forget, you'll have plenty of time to explore your own way of life after you leave home. While you are in junior and senior high school and are living with your parents, maybe you should try to play the game by their rules. Is it really too much to ask?

There is no need to make problems for your parents

You see, when you do things which within your developing set of values are really okay, but which you know violate the principles your parents live by, you put your parents in a real bind. They have their friends who are basically like they are and who are watching them and you with an eagle eye. When you run out of bounds according to your parents' seemingly antiquated thinking, your parents' friends notice and usually mention it to everybody they see. It's very embarrassing for your parents to say the least. Do you really think you have the right to let your parents provide for all your needs and at the same time make fools out of them in front of their friends? Your parents need their friends just like you do.

So think this over. While you are still living at home, maybe you should play it pretty much as they want you to. Formulate your values, but don't openly act strongly in opposition to the values of your parents. You owe them something, you know. In just a few years, you will be away from them, on your own. Then you can try out your own values without hurting those you love; but don't be surprised if you get in a mess when some of your values backfire on you and really foul you up. If they do, don't be foolish enough to continue with them. Back off and recoup. Rearrange and adjust until you have fashioned a system of values you will be willing to teach your children, because that time is coming. A value that you wouldn't be willing to teach your children, shouldn't become one of your own, because you will be teaching it to them either by what you say or by example.

23

You Can't Be Happy Without Sensible Values

A young couple had just been married in the early evening. After the wedding, they left on their honeymoon. They had driven a long way, and it was nearly midnight when they passed a beautiful luxurious motel. The groom looked sadly at the bride and said, "Wish we could stay in that swank place, but we just can't afford it. But don't worry, one of these days, we'll be rich. We'll stay in places like that, and I'll buy you a big diamond and a mink coat."

The bride replied, "Darling, we're rich now, because we have each other. But maybe you're right. One of these days we'll still be rich, and maybe we'll also have some money."

Don't let riches be your highest value

The apostle Paul had a young friend named Timothy; and it seems like Paul was always trying to teach Timothy how to live a full life, just like I'm trying to teach you. Here's what Paul said to

Timothy, "But godliness with contentment is great gain. For we brought nothing into this world, and it is certain we can carry nothing out. And having food and raiment let us be therewith content. But they that will be rich fall into temptation and a snare, and into many foolish and hurtful lusts, which drown men in destruction and perdition. For the love of money is the root of all evil; which while some coveted after, they have erred from the faith, and pierced themselves through with many sorrows."

I can assure you that your ideas concerning money and the things money will buy are going to be a very important part of whether or not you are happy. Our world is money-mad; but don't throw your life away grabbing for money. It can't possibly make you happy if you don't have some other much more important things.

We do have to have good educations, jobs, and enough money to hold our heads high. There is nothing wrong with staying up with the Jones's so long as you pick the right Jones's to try to stay up with.

We live in a different time from Timothy and Paul. Some of the things Paul said apply in principle but not in fact. He told the women to let their hair grow long because prostitutes in that day wore their hair short. He told Onesimus to be a good slave. He told the women not to talk in church and not to wear jewelry. All of these things apply in principle. This is what I meant in the last chapter when I talked about interpreting the Bible properly.

Aim high, but aim sensibly

What I want you to do is determine as best you can just what level of living makes sense for you to try and attain. I certainly don't want you to be a quitter. If you aim at something, I want you to go after it—that's been our suggestion all through this book. But choose your goals wisely.

If you shoot too high so far as money is concerned, you may become obsessed with money. It is easy to get caught in the "rat race" for money. You've got to figure sensibly how much money you want to make by considering where you start from, your intelligence, your parents' backgrounds, etc. I'll venture a guess that you can get filthy rich if you put your mind to it. But then, it might occupy all of your mind and energies; and you may wind up a broken old man with no one to care if you live or die.

You can't get to the top financially

Don't ever make the mistake of thinking about "getting to the top." There isn't any top. If you had fifty millions, you'd want sixty. If you count your success in life as having a dollar value, you'll never really have a feeling of success.

Put some value on the dollar—you have to. But think about other things too. Your family should mean more to you than money. Having time to be with and enjoy your wife and children is better than money—believe me, I know.

During the summer training camp, after I've been away from my family for about three weeks, there are many days when I feel like it isn't worth it. There I am so tired I could almost drop, hurting and sore from a hundred little bruises and a few big ones, dejected and beat. I think about my family down in Texas, and I'm just about ready to throw in the towel. Believe me, if it was just a matter of money with me, I would have thrown it in long ago.

Don't ask me right now why I play professional football—it's a long story. But let me tell you, my life is not built around money, and I don't want yours to be either.

Avoid the "rat race"

I think everyone of you will know what I mean when I say you should avoid the "rat races." This may or may not have a connection with money. I've seen people in the "rat race" who made fifty dollars a week, and I've seen some in the "rat race" who made five thousand dollars a week. One type was just as miserable as the other.

If a job doesn't include time for relaxation and enjoyment of life, it's not worth having. If you spend all your time making a living and never have time for really living, you're as good as dead.

You are all different. There are some of you that should be independent businessmen, and some who should work for a salary. Study yourselves carefully. Are you the kind who can have a business on your hands, maybe one that isn't doing too well, and who can leave it behind you when you go home to supper? Some can and some can't. If you are the worrying kind, you'd better leave the management to someone else.

For the guy who worries a lot, a salary is a mighty good way of life. You do your work, you leave at five o'clock and you forget the job until the next morning at eight. Maybe you don't make as much, but you live a lot more.

The worst thing for the worrier is a commission job. If you don't make a sale, you don't get a commission. Some guys just love it that way; others get ulcers. Again I say, study yourself carefully; and stay out of the "rat race." And remember, what is a "rat race" to one guy may be a great challenge to another.

Put pleasure in its place

There was an ancient group of Greek philosophers who called themselves the Epicureans. Their philosophy was "Eat, drink, and be merry, for tomorrow you may die." Maybe they had something.

Yes, there is something of good in this philosophy, but it's not the right way of life for a Christian. Enjoyment is fine, God wants us to enjoy our lives. If He had not, He wouldn't have created such a beautiful and wonderful place for us. The point is, He doesn't expect us to place pleasure in the center of our lives.

The Christian's life should be joyful, but it should be a life devoted to service. I want you to give a lot of thought to this, and place your values in the proper perspective. Put service first and pleasure second and you won't be far wrong.

Live the clean life

It has been said that "cleanliness is next to godliness." A lot of people think that this means cleanliness of the body only. But I want you to think of it in a different way. A clean life lived with good habits, pure thoughts, and lofty ideals is truly next to godliness. You don't have to be told what is clean and what is not.

One of the repulsive things you could drift into is the habit of cursing. A dirty mouth which spews obscenity and language of the gutter is filthy for a Christian or anybody else. This is the type of thing that can get to be a habit so easily. Keep your thoughts clean, because a dirty mouth is the result of a dirty mind.

You have to live in this world and you can't isolate yourself from some of the bad influences. Sometimes things happen on the job where you work—people tell dirty stories, and they use vile language. But your values must insist that you rise above this without your feeling you are better than they are.

I am sure you understand that some people do certain things which don't seem evil to them, because some things really are a matter of different values held by different people. For instance, drinking wine or beer with meals is something that many people do without thinking anything at all about it. It is not degrading, because their systems of values permit this type thing.

On the other hand, there are other things that are almost universally seen as degrading. Homosexuality, dope addiction, cowardice, adultery, murder, and mistreatment of old people are looked down on in almost any culture.

As a Christian you must go the second mile

As a Christian, you must develop your own value system and live by it. Even though you realize that all values aren't necessarily absolute, you realize that it is necessary to stand for something, even though the rightness or wrongness of these things may be debatable. Of course, sexual morality for the Christian is clearly set out in the Bible.

As a Christian, you must give your neighbors the right to their values. It is not necessarily your business to interfere with the lives of others beyond the point of showing them the better way as you see it. Again, you are not appointed to be a moral policeman. You can't really best help a person by jumping on his conduct; you must realize the reason he thinks differently is that he doesn't know the same people you do. He doesn't know your parents and friends, and above all, he may not know Christ. Your prime job is to introduce him to Christ. You aren't likely to do this if you constantly clobber him about his conduct.

As a Christian, you should be tolerant of the values of others, and you shouldn't look down on others as they try to do what they think is right.

Loyalty is important

Among the ideals that Christ has taught us, one of the most important is loyalty. You should be loyal to your church, your family, and to your country.

Your loyalty to your country should prevail over selfish interests unless it is a matter that violates your conscience. Today a lot of people are disloyal. We dare not say that all the people showing this disloyalty are bad, because it is possible that their consciences are being violated. But be careful that your resistance to any cause is not an excuse rather than a good reason for refusing to serve.

24

You and The Drinking Problem

Face the facts—thousands of lives are wrecked every year by alcohol. Some people will tell you that it isn't alcohol which wrecks these lives, that the drinking is a symptom of something deeper. This is partly true. The whole truth is that drinking is sometimes a symptom, and sometimes it is the drinking itself that is the basic problem.

Alcohol creates problems: it never solves them

You see, when drinking is a symptom of a deeper problem, the drinking becomes a barrier in the way of solving that problem. It provides an escape, thus causing the person to avoid facing up to the problem that's causing him to drink.

On the other hand, countless thousands of guys like you don't begin drinking in order to escape their problems, they begin because they feel that they must be a part of the "in group." What a mistake!

For you to start drinking just to show the boys you aren't a square is the most cowardly thing you'll ever do in your life.

This is giving in—proving yourself to be a real quitter. You must know that alcohol is likely to hurt or ruin you and the ones you love. If you go ahead anyway, you are not just a give-up guy, you are just flat stupid.

The thing is that drinking can be it's own problem. Once you get the habit, then you have a problem. Believe me, even if you didn't have one before, you have one now! But that's not the worst of it.

Drinking is like buying a false set of guts

It's pretty easy to see why some teen-agers drink. They do it because they don't want to be a "chicken," even though it's tougher to refuse than to accept. But to tell the truth, the guys aren't interested in logic or what's right or wrong. At the time, if you refuse, you're a drag. But sooner or later, they'll respect you for your guts. So you guys are often victims of what the crowd thinks, right or wrong. I understand that!

But did you ever stop to ask yourself the question, "Why do many of the girls drink?" Well, maybe they are influenced by the pressure of the crowd too, but if you'll think about it a minute or two, you will probably see that there's something else. Many guys and girls drink to prop up their sagging courage—to help them do what they really want to do and what they know is the wrong thing to do. Alcohol could be called a false set of guts.

Most teen-age sexual indulgence is preceded by drinking

You guys aren't blind. You get out to the parties. Maybe these parties are well chaperoned; the adults do the best they can. But everyone knows that the guys have bottles out in the cars; and they take their dates out to the car once in a while. By the end of the party some of them are loaded. The sponsoring adults are worried, but they don't quite know what to do. Or maybe, some of the better class kids wait until the party is over, and then they hit the bottle. They get pretty well looped before it's over with.

Now, why do they do this? Sometimes the boy gets the girl to drink in order to lower her moral resistance. They know that if she has had a few drinks she'll let them do some heavy petting. In some cases, the heavy petting leads to intercourse. This could happen without drinking, but it's much more likely with it.

Now, where does the liquor come in? The liquor gives them the courage (a false set of guts) to go ahead and make a fool of themselves. It gives the girls the courage to lose their virginity and to permit things they wouldn't even think of doing if they weren't a little drunk. And these are the nice kids who go to church and Sunday School. Surprisingly, many of them turn out all right in spite of all this. However, the chances of you ending up with a happy marriage with any girl with whom you have been on a drinking party are greatly lessened. Alcohol always distorts your judgment, and you could enter into a relationship with a girl when you and she are a little drunk that you wouldn't even think of entering into ordinarily. When you aren't drinking, you can at least see the girl without the distortion alcohol brings on.

Alcohol is the great deceiver

But what we are talking about is alcohol. The facts speak for themselves. Many guys and girls would remain sexually pure until marriage if it were not for alcohol. This drug, which minors aren't supposed to be able to buy, but which somehow they manage to get, makes fools out of people. It is the great deceiver. It makes you feel gay and bright when you are stumbling drunk and so stupid that you impose upon the love of your girl friend and push her into sex relations. What satisfaction could possibly come from such a relationship that vows love and trust, but which is really deceitful?

What could be more disgusting than to see an otherwise pretty and well-disciplined girl come apart at the seams, make disgusting passes at some jerk, and throw up all over the two of them while all the time she thinks she's cute?

They say social drinking is the accepted standard

Adults in our times are becoming more and more social drinkers. Many sensible people justify this by saying that alcohol is the great relaxer and sets people free from their inhibitions. It certainly does. The trouble is it doesn't stop at relieving the social inhibitions, making people more conversational.

We don't need to take the time in this book to talk about social drinking. For you guys, the time for this kind of party drinking is several years away. For the most part, alcohol is banned from your social affairs and rightly so. What we need to impress on you are the facts about the kind of drinking guys your age are likely to be tempted to get into. Now, you don't need to feel eaten up with guilt if you have taken a drink or two already—maybe most of you have. And I want to level with you, alcohol is not the kind of drug that reaches out and grabs you like a snake or even like some of the narcotics do. Alcohol is accepted in our society while heroin is illegal for everyone.

But that doesn't keep it from being a really dangerous thing for you. Just keep your eyes open, and you'll see the fools other people make of themselves; and you will know that it just isn't smart to mess around with it in any form—beer, wine, or liquor. You don't need it!

Alcohol causes many automobile accidents

Have you ever had a buddy who was killed or seriously injured in an automobile accident? I have. What a waste it is to see these young bodies all mangled, sometimes beyond recognition! How many of these wrecks are caused by the driver who had a few drinks? You don't know! I don't either.

But use your head. You've seen what a few drinks can do to a fellow behind a wheel. Even a little beer can seriously impair judgment and cause the driver to be reckless. Alcohol is the great liar. It makes a guy feel like he could drive a locomotive with one hand when really he would be dangerous driving a bicycle. When the gang gets to feeling pretty high, they yell, "Let's see you do ninety, Jim!" Then when they untangle the bodies, people blame the steering mechanism. Your reactions are slower when you've been drinking. You can't hit the brake fast enough. Even one bottle of beer slows the reaction time. There have been many times when I have missed a wreck by an inch. If I had had a bottle of beer, I hate to think what would have happened.

The liquor industry is out to get you

The liquor industry will go broke if they are unable to attract the youth of our country. Open your eyes and look at their advertising. They picture drinking as the thing the big man does. It's usually the very successful man, often surrounded by beautiful women, who is pictured in the advertisements. Their message is, "Look at this successful man—if you want to be like he is, you need brand X to serve to your guests."

Naturally, they don't show the pictures of the young high school girl throwing up or the twisted bodies of your friends being pulled out of the wrecked automobiles. You must have been at the scene of wrecks, or at least I'm sure you have seen the drivers' education films and pictures of wrecks caused by DWI.

For the sake of argument let's concede that social drinking by adults might not be all bad. Maybe it's a good social mixer. Even if it is—and I don't say it is—that doesn't mean that you should let it make a fool of you, ruin your life by robbing you of your good judgment, and causing you to disgrace yourself.

No one knows whether or not he will become an alcoholic

Technically the statisticians differentiate between the alcoholics and the problem drinkers. There are supposed to be several million alcoholics and several million problem drinkers in our country. Which will you be? Very likely neither, even if you do take up social drinking. We might as well be honest about it.

But you can't tell whether or not you are the kind of person who will become addicted to alcohol. Almost everyone would become addicted to heroin in a short time, but relatively few become true addicts to alcohol, because it is not as potent a drug as heroin. But you may be one of those who would become addicted. It has something to do with body chemistry which nobody really understands.

The thing is that you can't be an alcoholic if you don't drink. Why don't you join with the thousands of young men who have the courage to say "no" to alcohol. You don't need it for a successful life.

PART SIX

You and Your Sexuality

25

You Must Understand Your Sexual Nature

The modern world is completely aware that young people need information about themselves, their personalities, and the nature of their sexual drives. Much information is dispensed in school and at home. But, sometimes you can't get just the right information you want and need, so you continue to be puzzled and confused about certain matters pertaining to sex.

All males are pretty much alike, yet individually different, too

All males are pretty much alike in their sexuality. At the sight of an attractive female, especially if the female is trying to arouse the male's sexuality, the sex organs secrete hormones into the bloodstream and this mysterious feeling of sex arousal comes. If the stimulation is strong enough, the male organ becomes ready for sex relations with the female.

This readiness comes almost without conscious thought to young men who have reached the stage of puberty. The thing you should understand from this is that you are a normal young man and that your body is mature enough for the sex act. You shouldn't feel guilty about having sexual desire. This is perfectly natural.

But of course, since you aren't married and are probably too young to think of it for a while, you realize that you will just have to accept things are they are. You aren't free to indulge in the sex act. To do so would be very disastrous for a number of reasons.

The difference in males is that some are more easily aroused than others, and some have stronger feelings than others. Of course, it is hard for you to figure out whether your feelings are stronger than the other fellow's. You must realize that the stronger your natural feelings of sex are the closer you must guard against allowing yourself too much freedom either of thought or of action.

Your body can take care of itself

Some young men are persuaded that if their bodies respond to sexual stimuli and if they are ready for it physically, it will be bad for their health if they don't indulge one way or another either by having sex with a girl or by using one of the many ways available to bring about a climax.

It is true that your growing body provides the seminal fluid in your glands which is at least partly responsible for the feelings of sex. It is also true that your body will from time to time release some of this fluid. This varies a great deal from one fellow to another. Some guys have regular "wet dreams" in which these fluids are secreted in their sleep, others almost never do.

You may be certain that this is nature's way of taking care of your body. So, if you do have these wet dreams, you need feel no guilt about it; if you don't have them, your body is wise enough to know you don't need them. The fact that you have these dreams while indulging in some type of sexual play (in your dreams) is nothing for you to feel guilty about either.

You see, you are strictly responsible for control of your body and to some extent of your thoughts while you are in the waking state, but when you go to sleep, the censors go to sleep too and thoughts and impressions come on in your dreams which you can't control. Anyway, you may know for certain that these "wet dreams" are natural and that most guys have them.

There is nothing shameful about sexual feelings

You must know without a doubt that there is nothing at all shameful about sexual feelings. If you didn't have them you would be abnormal. At the same time, there may be some concern attached to the way you deal with these feelings. You must develop patterns of dealing with them that will bring about for you the highest possible happiness for you in your married life. You must deal with your feelings in a manner that will leave you no cause to be guilty.

There are few young men who have not experienced an ejaculation of semen at night while they slept, and there are few who have not in some manner stimulated themselves so as to bring about an ejaculation. As you know, any type of self-stimulation is called masturbation. If you have not done this at some time or other, you may have a right to be a little proud; but at the same time, it is nothing to be ashamed of if you have. On the other hand contrary to a lot of old wives' tales, it wouldn't endanger either your mental or physical health if you should continue.

Here is the mature way

But in the interest of your mature stature as a man, there are two things that you might wish to consider. First, it is in no way a mark of maturity to have sex with a woman before you are married. It is not an indication of strength but of weakness. Indulging is the weakling's way out. Keeping yourself pure is the hard way, the mature way, and the way of the strong-minded. Even if you should discount the possible harm you might do to the girl, it is not the thing a strong, mature man does.

Secondly, the best way to handle your sexuality before marriage regardless of whether it is a month from now or ten years is to let your body handle the problem automatically as you sleep. Make every effort to control the amount of stimulation you give your body through excessive petting and thought stimulation; don't be ashamed of being a man and experiencing feelings of a sexual nature when they come, but then just let nature take its course.

Sexual behavior is habit forming

You see, the need for sexual activity grows with experience. If you masturbate, it will become a habit that will likely enslave you against your will. You will likely have to continue it if you have really let it become a habit. You will have to undergo a sense of self-devaluation every time you do it, because you know it isn't the mature thing for a man to do. So the ideal is to become involved in so many other things that you live a full life without sexual indulgence until time for your marriage.

The same thing applies to sexual promiscuity with women. Even if the woman you have relations with is already a prostitute and is therefore not hurt by it, this action will fast become a habit which you will not be able to break, and you will degrade yourself in your own eyes every time you do it. More than that, such actions get in the way of your normal love life with the girl who will some day mean so much to you. If you get in the habit of sex relations with girls who are not really hurt by it before you fall in love, you will be prone to pressure the girl you love into a relationship which will undermine your whole future.

Surely you know that sexual indulgence with the girl you are going to marry is very dangerous. Chances are you will love her too much to wish to degrade her and to ruin your chances of complete happiness later. The possibility of pregnancy and forced marriages hovers over untold thousands of young couples who just couldn't wait. This is a horrible way to start a marriage.

You are the protector of the one you love

The sexual drive of most men is stronger than that of most women. There are individual cases where this isn't true at all, but it is best to judge it to be that way. At the same time, girls are more romantic by nature and they often will allow a great deal of intimacy believing that there is no danger. You should know how far to go without getting into the danger zone. It is almost paradoxical that girls are slower to be aroused, they enjoy the romantic caresses more, and yet when they are swept along too far on the wings of their emotions they turn out to be almost powerless.

The point is that the man must draw the line because in our society he is the aggressor in love. It is up to you to see that your petting doesn't get out of hand.

Some girls are very aggressive sexually

At this point, you have been made aware that most girls are slower to be stimulated sexually than most men. Earlier it was agreed that women are special creatures who need our honor and protection.

But you should face all of the truth, not just part of it. There are some women who are highly sexed and who are able to lead a young man to a point of no return. Although these are in the minority, you must be aware that there are some like that.

Many young men have been seduced by over-sexed girls who just wanted a good time. The lives of these young men have been ruined because with these women they have developed a promiscuous sex habit.

Most men who maintain their purity until marriage are very happy with the sex lives they lead with their wives. On the other hand, the record shows that men who develop promiscuous sex lives before marriage are unlikely to be happy within the framework of monogamous marriage. They have played the field; and they may never be able to put it out of their minds completely, no matter how fine a home they have. You are going to expect your wife to be faithful to you, but you shouldn't expect it unless you are faithful to her. Don't disqualify yourself from having this kind of fair play in marriage by developing habits that make it unlikely if not impossible. This is just another of the many reasons why you must remain sexually pure until your marriage.

26

Your Sex Drive Is Natural

In God's plan for His world, every form of life must be maintained and replenished; each living thing reproduces so that life may go on. For this reason, God has endowed all his creatures at least at the mammalian level with a sex drive. This is a powerful and rather mysterious drive activated by hormones secreted into the blood stream by the sex glands; this is the reason for your attraction to the opposite sex.

There's good reason to believe that the sex drive in animals has just one purpose, reproduction. Whatever pleasures animals derive from the sex act is likely to be for nature's purpose of insuring continuing offspring and is accompanied by immediate gratification so far as animals are concerned. Man is unique in that not only does he get immediate pleasure and release from the sex act, but he's able to use this act as a means of expressing love and bringing pleasure to his wife.

Sex has purposes other than reproduction

It is clear that sexual behavior for man has many purposes beyond that of reproduction. It is also clear that God's plan for you involving matters of love, affection, companionship, pleasure in sex, and reproduction revolves around family life. In other words, He intends that one man is for one woman for life to share the good and the bad together.

God made the male animals capable of reproducing through sex relations with many females; but he made the female animals capable of performing the sex act only at certain specified times when the females are capable of reproducing. Thus, sex for the animal is solely for the purpose of reproduction. A female dog is only "in heat" and capable of the sex act and reproduction about twice a year; the cow only once a year.

But God made the female human capable of sexual relations almost any time, whether or not her body is ready for reproduction. Thus, God made a mate for man who could share his sexual desires at all times, making the principle of one man for one woman logical and reasonable.

Sex is the biggest problem of youth

Several studies in which high school youth were asked to state their biggest problem has suggested that popularity or being accepted by the group is the number one problem of American youth. However, at a recent meeting of young women who were competing for the Miss Teen-Age America contest, this question was answered honestly by several of the young ladies who confessed that sex is the biggest current problem of young people.

This isn't surprising, and yet you might wonder just why sex has become such a problem for young people. There are several important reasons. According to these girls, it wasn't a matter of sex relationships or no sex relationships that made the problem acute. The constant question was, "How far should I go in making love to my boy friend?"

Animals probably experience no sex problems. When a female is "in heat" she seeks the attentions of any available male, both female and male are satisfied by the sex act and that is all there is to it. The male animal, on the other hand, probably doesn't experience strong sex urges unless his emotions are excited by having a female "in heat" come near. Then he fulfills the drive and forgets it until the next time a female who is ready for the sex act approaches him.

You are at the mercy of nature and culture

But human beings have many problems, especially the unmarried young people. Your sex drives are constant, and because of your tremendous brain power you are able to think about the attractiveness of that special girl. As a matter of fact, you are to some degree forced into a constant state of excitement because our culture splashes sex symbols all around you. You will also remember that unlike the female animal who only desires sex once or twice a year, the female human is able to be sexually stimulated at almost any time.

This is a part of the problem. But even worse, our culture has made it almost impossible for young people who fall in love to marry for several years after their sex urges have reached a peak. They must fight the battle of self-control constantly over a period of years.

Then, too, because of man's brainpower, because he isn't permitted to indulge his sex feelings, and because our society has placed many taboos on sex, he has concocted many schemes for satisfying his urges in deviant ways. A young man may have sexual experiences in many ways other than sex relations with a woman. Chief among these means are masturbation and homosexuality.

You guys make jokes about some of your buddies being "queers." It's really no laughing matter. Some unfortunate people become homosexuals because of psychological reasons which are so complex that even the best psychiatrists haven't figured out what causes it. Mostly, it is something that happens during the first few years of life.

There is a lot of difference between a homosexual who is that way because of things that happened when he was a child and one who gets that way through foolish actions during the teen-age years.

Some of you have fooled around with sex with another guy during the early years of adolescence. No need to give up in despair about it if you have.

But let me warn you: You could keep on with this pattern until it kind of "gets in your blood." The point is, you can become a homosexual starting out from having mutual masturbation with boys when you are a teen-ager. You wouldn't be a psychological homosexual; you would just get the habit of preferring boys to girls. You would still be making a big mess of your life, and you can't afford to do it.

God's plan for human sexual behavior

It is virtually universally agreed that God's plan for man's sex life is to have him remain a virgin until he falls in love with a woman who then becomes his wife. In the Christian home, sex behavior for pleasure and reproduction is good and it is healthy. Many young people follow God's plan, and they're never sorry for maintaining their sexual purity until marriage. Admittedly, the cultural demand for later marriages creates many hardships and hazards, but the plan of God is always best. Although you may find it hard to do, you must yield to God's plan and to some extent to cultural demands if you are to be happy.

You can't afford to marry too young for at least two reasons. First, you must be emotionally mature enough to be ready for marriage. In your infatuation and because of your lack of experience in getting to know many girls, you could easily make an unfortunate mistake. When you are in love with a girl, it's hard to see her as she really is.

In the second place, you must have achieved a level of education and job-readiness that would make it possible for you to make a living. There are two strikes against your marriage to start with if you have to accept money from your parents. It isn't fair to them. And it tends to cause great friction between you and them. So the sensible plan for your life is to control your sexual urges until you are ready for marriage, have found a girl you love, and have married her. A teen-age marriage according to statistics has relatively little chance for success.

You are partners with God in the creative process

You should always remember that God has endowed you with the capacity to join with Him and with another human of opposite sex in the creating of new life. The sex act is primarily designed for this purpose, but man has been given the further privilege to use sex in marriage to express his deep love for his wife. This is pleasurable, and binds them ever closer to each other. Sexual relations in marriage do much to make the relationship happy and sustaining for both husband and wife. Sexual indulgences before marriage unavoidably bring guilt and heartaches. It is unlikely that sex relations before marriage are ever really satisfying.

The girl is seldom if ever gratified because she always wonders if she's the first. Also it is usually done in an atmosphere not suited to guilt-free expression of real love. It is more like animal passion. Whatever immediate pleasures you may possibly have pale into total insignificance when compared to the destruction of trust and future happiness. Regardless of what people are saying in defense of the "new morality," the "sex revolution" is losing steam because young people are coming to realize that guilt and heartache are inevitable with loose morals. Sexual license doesn't really bring the fulfillment young people expect.

There is another problem that you ought to think about also and that is the possibility of getting your girl friend pregnant. In an address at Baylor University, Dr. Henry Bowman, a noted authority on sex and marriage, compared premarital sexual intercourse with playing Russian roulette. It's one thing if you're stupid enough to put the gun to your head and pull the trigger, but when you point it at someone else, that's a different story. If you love your girl friend, you won't play Russian roulette by pointing a gun at her. That's about what you do in premarital intercourse.

PART SEVEN

You and The Opposite Sex

27

Girls Are Fun

During the last few years, I've been talking to guys like you all over the United States in all kinds of meetings. I've found that most of you are interested in sports, but that *all* of you are interested in girls.

Being a normal young man, your relationships with women will be wide and varied. But your relationships with girls of your own age is really a subject of special interest for you. In fact, you will spend a great deal of time with girls from now on. This is an important thing chiefly because your choice of a girl to live with for the rest of your life is probably one of the two or three most important decisions of your entire life.

Every girl you meet is a possible choice as a life partner

Getting to know girls whether in dating or chance relationships is such a pleasant thing for a guy that you may not want to take a serious look at it at all. Knowing girls really makes life worth living, and I don't want to take away from the fun of it by making you think too seriously about it.

At the same time, you are interested in building your life not just for immediate pleasures and joys but for the future also. As I said, you'll choose your wife from among the girls you are around a lot or at least from the ones with whom you have social contact. There is a sense in which all contacts with the opposite sex point toward choosing a wife. Just tuck that away in the back of your mind; such a thought shouldn't interfere with your having a good time.

You should be having fun

Luckily for you, you can have a lot of fun with a girl even though you know that in the back of both her mind and yours the idea of finding a mate is inescapable. You should get to know a lot of girls. It's more fun that way, and your chances of ultimately choosing the right one will be much greater.

But for now, you can let wife selection slide; even though it's really important, it's a thing of the future. You shouldn't begin to think too seriously about marriage until after you complete your education. You ought to have a lot of serious thoughts, but don't miss having a good time. And some of the best times a guy can have are likely to be with spirited and lovely young women.

There is a tremendous wide-open world of fun you can have—fun that you can have with no regrets and no guilt. On the other hand, there are some things people are likely to call fun which leave a Christian worried and confused. It's a pity that so many choose the kind of fun that hurts themselves and others rather than the wholesome fun that livens up everyone. At least a large part of these mistakes are made from not knowing rather than from not caring. It's up to you not only to know but to care—as a Christian you really have no choice.

The more girls the more fun, at least in the early stages

Our society doesn't condone early marriages. There are various reasons for this, and many of them are very good. So it's best for you to date many girls. This way you can get to know a lot of girls and have fun with all of them. You don't become tied down to one person and miss a lot of good times you could have with many different girls.

Steady or not, get out and have fun

The important thing is not the question of going steady; it is that you really do get out and go. Sure, you have various obligations and you don't want to be going constantly; but you don't want to be a drag either. Get your studying done, do what your parents ask you to do, take care of your part-time job; but save some time for living it up. You won't be young but once. Fun doesn't need to stop when you get married either; but any way you look at it, you are wasting time if you are a stick-in-the-mud.

Social affairs are designed with you in mind

Various groups go to a lot of trouble arranging social affairs for young people. Those who work so hard are often disappointed.

They often moan, "When we have something for them, they just don't come." Maybe some of these affairs aren't so great, but if they aren't, it seems reasonable that the sponsors would welcome suggestions for their improvement.

The point is that too many of you are turning away from social life much of the time if not completely. Don't forget that your happiness depends upon your ability to develop as a social animal; and these affairs are the best growing ground you will have.

You should be a joiner

Our society is becoming more and more a series of particular groups. You must learn to handle yourself in many different groups. You should grab every opportunity you have for joining clubs, political groups, and service-minded organizations.

In these groups, especially those sponsored by your school and church, you will have many opportunities to work with people of both sexes. These groups are a good place to meet a lot of girls of the type worth dating.

There was a time during my first two years in high school that I really hated to ask a girl for a date. I really did enjoy going with them after I gathered the guts to ask them the first time. To tell the truth, I would have rather faced a fullback thirty pounds heavier than I, charging like a wild bull than a one hundred pound high-school beauty. The thing that helped me most to overcome this girl fright was meeting them in clubs and at social events in school or church.

If you are like I was and find it a little tough to make a direct approach to a girl, meeting her in a cooperative venture with a church-related or school group often breaks the ice for you; so in order to come in contact with a lot of girls, you should be a joiner.

How to ask a girl for a date

God made man and woman to complement each other. Any man who can be happy all the time without the company of a woman is abnormal. Yet, the possibility of getting the most from being around the opposite sex is a matter of self-training. You won't really fully enjoy being around girls unless you practice.

For most of you, getting along with the opposite sex is just as natural as breathing. If you're like that, you're fortunate. But maybe you feel uncomfortable around them; you aren't as relaxed as you are around the "ole gang." Maybe you are shy and prone to just giggle and act stupid, causing them to think you're immature or silly. What you need to do is pick out a girl you really want to date and imagine yourself walking boldly up to her and asking her for a date. Imagine her to say, "Oh, I'd love to, but I've already got a date tomorrow night." Don't give up, just proceed by saying, "Well, I don't give up easily, how about Saturday night?" See her accepting excitedly. Do this several times before you ask her. The very next time you see her, just ask away. It won't be long until it'll come naturally.

Choose girls who are compatible with you

There are a lot of girls in the world, and most of them have a lot of good things about them. But some are better suited for you than others and you are better suited for them. When I suggest that you be selective in whom you date, I'm not suggesting that you be a stuck-up snob. You'll have more fun with the girls with whom you have the most in common. This means your family backgrounds socially, economically, and religiously should be similar. It's a real waste to date a girl who is incompatible with you socially or religiously when there are so many available that are like you.

Many of you are making the mistake of dating girls you know you wouldn't be happy with should the association lead to marriage. This isn't smart, because you never know when your infatuation for each other may grow and your wish to be together may grow into a love relationship.

If marriage is walking hand in hand down life's pathway, then you shouldn't consider walking separately in the spiritual life. That's the most important area. If you get friction here, it'll rub you raw. The same problems may also develop because of social or economic differences, though they aren't as crucial as the spiritual friction.

This is also the problem involved in a marriage between two people of different races. There's likely to be much friction. Then too, there will be the added problem of the children really not being accepted by either race, not to mention the couple being rejected socially in many cases.

You say, "But look, I'm just dating. I'm not even thinking of mariage." I say, "Play it safe; date only those girls with whom you would be glad to spend the rest of your life if things should work out that way." There are just too many girls around to make it worth taking a chance. I know this is tough to see now, but marriage is for life. You should have as much in common as possible.

Investigate the reputations of the girls you date

One of your most prized possessions is your reputation. Once your reputation is fouled up, even when you weren't responsible, it's very hard to reestablish. You are known by the girls you date. You can't escape this and you shouldn't try.

It may be all right to have a passing acquaintance with girls whose reputations aren't good; they may be in the same groups that you're in. And sometimes these girls are prone to push themselves at you. Not wishing to offend them you may almost get trapped into dating them. You should be very careful of this; you shouldn't date a girl whose reputation is questionable. At the same time don't be self-righteous.

If you date a morally sloppy girl, the sharp, wholesome girls will be suspicious of you. You will lose friends of both sexes, young and old. It just isn't worth the price. The fact that you may keep yourself and your behavior beyond reproach doesn't make much difference. Again, you are known by the girls you date. As a Christian, your responsibility is greater than that of the non-Christian. Remember you represent Christ. Does your behavior in all things show Christian ideals to the world?

As sensible as this sounds, I know that many of you narrow down the field and fall into the trap of going steady. There sure are a lot of you who do it, and there are some good things about it. It gives you the security of always knowing you can have a date with a girl you like to be with. Don't forget that the security is mostly for the girl's benefit, because she can't openly ask for a date. So she pressures you in little ways; and in order to please her, you agree to go steady.

Some of you guys don't have the guts to brave new frontiers. You'd just rather stick with the same girl. You don't want the frightening experience of asking another girl for that first date. You'd be surprised, it may be exciting and fun. Remember this will be the only time that God or man will really condone your playing the field. There'll be a time soon enough when you must settle down to one girl. You really can't know for sure that you'll get the best mate possible, unless you've dated enough girls to know how to judge. But then it is true that you could be just yielding to the built-in inclination of human beings—you are adopting the God-given concept of one man for one woman at too early an age.

You should be aware of the advantages of playing the field as opposed to going steady. If you know the reasons for doing this, and you still feel that your greatest happiness as a young person comes from going steady, then it is just a case of choosing with full knowledge of the possible disadvantages. You have chosen, and you are man enough to accept the consequences both good and bad.

(I know you're thinking it, so I'll say it for you, "It's really your own business.")

28

You Must Be The Protector

If the girl you date doesn't deserve your full concern for her welfare, you shouldn't be going out with her. As corny as it might seem, there is a sense in which the mature young man must assume the role of protector of women, especially when he asks a girl for a date. You have to realize the parents' attitude toward their daughter. All her life they've cared for and protected her with great love. Now you come along and ask her for a date. The parents are saying when they agree to let you date her, "Now you are her protector." They depend on you to bring her back safely. Physically and emotionally you are responsible for her.

I didn't really understand this until four years ago when I became the father of a little girl. Since then I have protected her from everything including the neighbor's dog and her own brothers. And if you should come along in ten years and try to get a date with her, then, ole partner, you'd better be ready to take care of her, because right then I'd be turning over my job to you.

If you do the job fine! But if you don't, you've "had it." Seriously, it won't be long until you'll have a little darling like mine and you'll probably be worse than I am. You'll pet her more than you'll pet that first new car.

The display of intimacies is a natural thing

Intimacies between young men and young women are natural, and can be entirely wholesome. On the other hand, these intimacies can quickly get out of hand. During courtship you must be not only well-informed but well disciplined.

The problem of intimacies is one of the reasons why it's best that you not date a certain girl steadily until you are ready for marriage, or at least for engagement. The more you are together, the easier it is for things to get out of hand unless one of you has firm self-control. In our society there is something of a paradox here. It's usually the girl that is expected to draw the line to keep the boy from "going too far." The paradox is that few girls are really equipped for this task. Girls are very romantic and are as a rule easily swept off their feet. They can be swept along in a wave of romanticism that allows forms of petting that are dangerous. They become so engrossed in the romance of petting that they may be quite unaware of the dangers which come when the boy becomes overly excited. They think they have control, when as a matter of fact they don't.

You may be sure that nine-tenths of the "mistakes" young people make are based on the assumption on the part of the boy that the girl will exercise her sense of control and won't allow certain progressive petting practices before the real danger point is reached. Thinking she can control, the girl suddenly finds her romantic feelings surging into truly sexual feelings and her sense of control is swept away. The young man relying on the cultural rule that the girl is the one to say "no," regrettably "goes too far."

The sensible thing from your point of view is to assume the role of protector. It's not a criticism of the young women you go out with that the control is really in your hands. But for safety's sake, you must develop the habit of thinking of yourself as the one who determines what is safe and what isn't.

Since the male is the aggressor, he must be the protector

In our culture, the male is the aggressor in matters of intimacies and love making. Most young men don't like aggression on the part of the female, and the girls have generally conceded the point. If you are the aggressor, then obviously you must be the one who exercises self-control. It is too much to ask of girls that they submit to your advances and that they maintain a position of control. Only you can control your drive; some girls will feel they love you so much that they will permit you to overstep all reasonable boundaries. The pitiful young woman who was used by a male usually cries, "I loved him so much that I just couldn't find it in my heart to say no."

It's definitely best for you to know that many girls won't deny you. The problem is that society has asked them to exercise the kind of self-control that only the male aggressor can handle.

There are some aggressive girls around, too

With all of this said, we do need to concede that there are some girls who are very aggressive. It's not correct to say, "Beware of these." They may be fine girls, they may have grown up in a family where open expression of love was encouraged, or they may be strongly sexed. None of this is bad in itself; but at the same time, you do need to be more on your guard with this type girl. When her aggressiveness is added to your naturally strong sex drive, things can get out of hand in a hurry.

It's really too bad that the girls who present the greatest dangers during courtship are the same ones who reasonably will make fine wives, at least insofar as open expression of love in marriage is concerned.

You must be fair with the girls you date

Many of you have fallen into the habit of heavy petting. Most of you don't intend to go to dangerous lengths; however, many of you do so in spite of your intentions. You should carefully consider the dangers of heavy petting, even that engaged in with the full intent of control. Sure, some young couples manage to engage in such petting for a long time, perhaps for years without a tragic slip.

Heavy petting isn't really a satisfying relationship. It can be especially unhealthy and disturbing to the young woman. Ask yourself the question, "Do I really have the right to expect my date to take part in heavy petting that leaves her frustrated, nervous, and guilty?" The practice of heavy petting brings frustration and guilt more to girls than to boys.

It is better to find other things to do

A young couple that takes every opportunity to be alone so they may engage in petting is definitely taking a chance of warping their personalities. The entire thing usually results in frustration, since marriage and therefore complete fulfillment sexually is usually impractical until after college. It's just smart to maintain a greater and more comfortable distance from each other during dating years.

You should be out doing things with other young people. You can go to parties and social events of all kinds, rather than running away to hide in a quiet place and pushing the limits of your endurance. Paul says to young Timothy in the Bible, "Flee youthful lusts." So should you. It's not that you aren't all man with a strong sex drive—you know what love and sex are all about. It's your choice to wait until it's the right time rather than to take chances with your happiness for the sake of some thrills which leave you feeling guilty at best. This is really best for you and the girl. This doesn't mean that you can't express your feelings at all; it will probably mean that the good night kiss will be given at the end of the date rather than over a prolonged period in the parked car.

You should allow for some progression of intimacies

It makes sense that the longer you are around a girl, especially if you feel you are in love with her, the more intimate you are going to become. For this reason, you must be sure to leave room for a progression of intimacies. If you engage in heavy petting from the beginning of your romance, there is only one direction you can go. And if the only thing that's left is intercourse to complete the development of intimacies, there is going to be a tremendous strain on your control system.

So many fine young people who love each other very much are forced into marriage too early simply because they can't control their emotions. If you are really in love with a girl, you don't want to let anything spoil your life with her as your wife. You should know that marriage before either of you is ready for it will spell disaster and strained relationships all the way through your lives.

So, be smart. Heavy petting doesn't prove you are manly and strong. Quite the contrary, it proves you are weak and stupid. You are much too smart to take chances with your own life and that of the girl you love.

A Word From Stan Moser

Now is my chance to come right out and say a personal word to each and every one of you.

I have read this book many times during the preparation of the manuscript, and I am certainly thrilled at having had the opportunity to contribute some of my own ideas. I am a senior in high school, and feel that as a result of this joint effort with my father and Bill Glass I have become a better person.

You can't work with a guy like Bill Glass for three months and not learn to appreciate his genuine, sincere feeling for young people. He understands us; and he has tried the best he knows how to put things in the pages of this book that will help you and me to live a better life in the eyes of God, our own selves, and our fellow men.

While working on this book, I feel that I have come face to face with the problems of a young man growing into mature adulthood. Keeping all these things in mind, I have studied these pages far more intensely than any of you ever will. For this reason, I feel that I can honestly suggest that the ideas in this book will really work for *you,* and I can endorse every word one hundred percent.

We must all strive toward a more perfect life, keeping in mind when we fail that none of us will ever be as perfect as Christ was and is; but we can all learn to stand tall and straight as true Christians seeking God's goal for our lives.

Stan Moser

Enjoy Life!

I really hope you have a great game, or should I say a great life. I know that the world will be a better place just because you've been around. I pray that you'll check in with the Great Coach of the universe—no man ever stands quite so tall and straight as when he bows his knees to the Creator.

When this short game is over, I hope you can say, *"I was a winner. I stood tall and straight, and I found God's design for a man."*

Oh yes! Best of all, there's still another big game coming up. This one lasts *forever*.

Bill